A–Z of Inclu
Early Childl

CW00818847

Mary Dickins

Mc Graw Hill Education Open University Press

Open University Press
McGraw-Hill Education
McGraw-Hill House
Shoppenhangers Road
Maidenhead
Berkshire
England
SL6 2QL

email: enquiries@openup.co.uk
world wide web: www.openup.co.uk

and Two Penn Plaza, New York, NY 10121-2289, USA

First published 2014

A catalogue record of this book is available from the British Library

ISBN-13: 978-0-335-24678-6
ISBN-10: 0-335-24678-8
eISBN: 978-0-335-24679-3

Library of Congress Cataloging-in-Publication Data
CIP data applied for

Typeset by Aptara Inc., India

Praise for this book

"Mary Dickins has given us a book which is a beautifully written guide to the principles and practice of inclusion in young children's care and education. For some this will be an introduction to, for others a reminder of, knowledge and skills which we have developed over many years but which are too often misunderstood or ignored. Through her alphabetical approach it is possible to address a huge number of issues in a very accessible way, either dipping into it as needed or reading from beginning to end as a story of how we can improve the experiences of young children in childcare, and every entry comes with a list of references to enable readers to take the subject further. Informing the whole book is her knowledge and experience of this issue and her passion to support the development of a shared vision and understanding of it. As she says: 'inclusion is not a fixed state…we all have responsibility and a role to play in challenging discrimination and oppression'."

—Sue Owen, Independent early years consultant

"I have learnt a lot from reading this book – and there is a lot to learn! Its scope is so enormous that inevitably it cannot cover everything, for example my pet topic of 'the power of assumptions'! It identifies the complexities of the various aspects of inclusion and touches on the inter-relatedness of many – for example, race and class. As readers dip into it I hope it will trigger further reading on particular issues and also stimulate more discussion of how institutional procedures and practices, deeply embedded in our society (the 'system'), remain barriers to inclusion. We all need to identify, understand and break down such barriers so that every one of our precious children, wherever they are, feel they truly belong."

—Jane Lane, Advocate worker for racial equality in the early years

"Mary Dickins has long experience in early years and equality issues and writes from a defined value system. She encourages a proactive and anti-discriminatory approach which contributes to the development of - in her words - 'a shared vision, understanding and sense of purpose'. Mary stresses the importance of individual responsibility and transfer of specialist skills to a mainstream context. This book is a good addition to the continuing debate on inclusion from a clear children's rights perspective and a valuable resource for the early years sector, providing a framework to embed effective inclusive practice."

—Julie Jennings, Royal National Institute of Blind People, UK

For my children Hannah and Theo

Contents

Terms used in this book

The term 'early years practitioner' is used to describe all those who directly care for and educate young children, including childminders and nannies.

The term 'early years setting' is used to describe any provision where young children are to be found.

The terms 'disabled child' or 'disabled children' are the preferred terms of reference because this is the terminology that disabled people have chosen. It is not the intention to define children in terms of what society sees as their shortcomings. The term 'disabled' is used positively and forcefully by the disability movement to indicate pride and this is respected here.

The term 'special educational need' is used because it is the wording of the relevant legislation and guidance.

Figures

Photographs

Acknowledgements

I would like to thank all the brilliant early years practitioners, managers, trainers, support staff and other professionals that I have met and worked with all over the country; especially my Early Childhood Studies students and colleagues at London Metropolitan University. You have all taught me so much and reminded me of how much I have still to learn. A special thank you to the children, staff and parents at Bemerton and Golden Lane Children's Centres for allowing me to invade their space and take the photographs that enrich and enliven the pages of this book. Thanks to Ruth Thomson and colleagues at Nursery World who first gave me the opportunity to develop some of these ideas in the series A–Z of Inclusive Practice. Thanks to my husband and my children for their tolerance and support and to my daughter Hannah Dickins and her friend Natalie Taylor for the production of the figures. Thanks to the Early Childhood Forum at the National Children's Bureau for the inspirational definition of inclusion which provides the framework for the discussions in this book. Thanks to the Young Children's Voices Network, also at the National Children's Bureau, for the adaptation of the figure of the Listening Cycle and to Sue Owen for the extracts from the Participation and Belonging Conference Report. Thanks to all the academics, writers, thinkers, campaigners, researchers and organisations from whose insights and hard work I have drawn. Thanks to Jane Lane for her knowledge, wisdom and friendship as well as her case study. Finally, thanks to my editor, Fiona Richman, for her patience and understanding.

- Photographs from Bemerton Children's Centre: Intro 1, B1, B2, C1, C2, F1, F2, G1, J1, K1, L1, R1, S2, S3
- Photographs from Golden Lane Children's Centre: A3, B3, D1, D2, J2, P1, S1, Z1
- Figures were designed by Mary Dickins apart from Figure L2, The Listening Cycle, which has been adapted courtesy of the Young Children's Voices Network at the National Children's Bureau.
- The practice examples are fictional but drawn from direct experience.

Introduction

> Inclusion is a process of identifying, understanding and breaking down the barriers to participation and belonging.
>
> (Early Childhood Forum 2003)

The definition of inclusion above was developed by the Early Childhood Forum (ECF) at the National Children's Bureau in 2003. The ECF brings together national organisations and professional associations in the early childhood sector to debate issues, celebrate differences and develop consensus to champion high-quality experiences for young children and their families. It aims to promote inclusion and challenge inequality.

This definition underpins the approach that has been taken to the issues and challenges described in this book. It represents a shift in thinking and a recognition that although inclusion was originally conceived of in relation to disabled children and those with other forms of special educational need, this is only part of the picture and that inclusive practice, policy and principles need to be applicable to all children regardless of any of the differences between them. Here you will find an interpretation of inclusion that is based on a defined value system that equally welcomes, celebrates and respects diversity arising from gender, race, ethnicity, language, culture, belief systems, socio-economic or family background, and level of educational disadvantage or disability. This is underpinned by an acceptance that inequality, racism, disablism and other forms of prejudice and discrimination are deeply embedded in today's society. From this perspective, promoting inclusion in the early years demands a proactive and anti-discriminatory approach that manifests itself in all aspects of principles, policy and practice.

The purpose of this book is to consider how the early years sector, as a whole, can better understand the concept of inclusion and successfully establish, examine and evaluate the building blocks and framework that should underpin inclusive practice. It is hoped that it will be of interest and value to anyone who wishes to increase their knowledge and understanding of these issues which often divide us as a society; especially in terms of the potential impact on young children and their families. The scope of this book is so enormous that no doubt there are relevant issues that have been neglected or skimmed over. Nevertheless, it represents a genuine attempt to identify the challenges and barriers to inclusion for all children; to understand them and in some measure to suggest how they might be overcome.

First, there are some achievements to celebrate. In the last 20 years we have seen huge progress towards a more socially inclusive model of education in many countries including the UK and much good practice has been conceived and consolidated. The concept is now also embedded in the policy documents of numerous international organisations including the United Nations Convention on the Rights of the Child (UNCRC; UNICEF 1989) which affirms the rights of all children to be treated equally and to be educated without discrimination. Currently, there is a consensus on the importance of early childhood in relation to children's future life chances, social inclusion and later citizenship. Furthermore, this view has been supported by a plethora of legislation and guidance including the Every Child Matters initiative (DfES 2003) which expressed the aim that every child, whatever their background or circumstances, should have the support they need to be healthy; to stay safe; to enjoy and achieve; to make a positive contribution and to achieve economic well-being. Despite a recent shift away from the terminology of the Every Child Matters agenda, these aims are arguably still embedded in the four recently revised Early Years Foundation Stage principles (DfE 2012a) that continue to recognise the uniqueness of every child; the need for positive relationships; the importance of enabling environments and the different rates and ways in which children develop and learn. New legislation promises earlier identification and support for families (DfE 2012b).

In order to understand the current picture, it is helpful to consider inclusion in its historical context. Inclusion has been high on the educational agenda since the Green Paper *Excellence for All Children* (DfEE 1997) signalled government commitment to the principle of including disabled children in mainstream services. The Special Educational Needs and Disability Act 2001 (Great Britain Parliament 2001) and the Disability Discrimination Act 1995 (DDA) (DfES 2002) combined to give a stronger right to mainstream education in the early years, making it clear that where parents want a mainstream place for their child, everything possible should be done to provide it. This mirrored the changes that were taking place in schools and other services. These were landmarks in a long campaign by many parents, professionals and disabled people against the practice of segregating children into special schools. However, the lack of a definition in law and guidance has meant that there are a perplexing variety of interpretations on offer and over the years the term has been defined in many different ways.

Nutbrown and Clough (2006: 3), for example, suggest that inclusion can be seen as 'the drive towards maximal participation in and minimal exclusion from early years settings, from schools and from society'.

The campaigning group Alliance for Inclusive Education has defined inclusive education as that which 'enables all students to fully participate in any mainstream early years provision, school, college or university' (Dickins with Denziloe 2003: 21).

While the first definition suggests that efforts should be made, the second is far more uncompromising. Nutbrown and Clough (2006: 3) observe that 'it is clear that there are as many "versions" of inclusion as there are early years settings – or, indeed the individuals who make up those particular cultures of living and learning'.

It is this lack of a common understanding and purpose that led (Rustemier 2004: 23) to state:

> While many more people now seem to be speaking the language of inclusion – social cohesion, community cohesion, racial integration, human rights, disability rights, rights to mainstream – what is happening in practice is much more muddled. 'Inclusion' has come to mean almost everything but the elimination of exclusion.

Rustemier certainly has a point. It is clear that there is no real consensus about what inclusion is and what it really means in practice. A primary concern of this book is that we cannot progress effectively without a shared vision and understanding. Confusion exists in particular about whether inclusion can or should embrace all forms of difference and how it is different from previous ideas about 'mainstreaming' and 'integration', which arguably remain embedded in psychological, educational, social and political contexts.

Using the ECF definition and the UNCRC as a framework, inclusion in the early years can be properly understood as an ongoing process by which all young children may be enabled to receive care and education in mainstream settings and are enabled to join in as fully as possible with their peers in the curriculum and life of the setting and in society. This process demands and expects the fullest possible participation of all children within all areas of activity within every provision. It also seeks to ensure that the quality and coherence of the care and education provided is fully commensurate with the needs and entitlements of the individual child and their family.

Also inherent to this definition is the recognition that barriers to inclusion and equality are to be found at individual and institutional levels. The implication is that if the 'barriers to participation and belonging' were identified and removed this would result in more equitable and inclusive service provision with the goal of providing a genuinely enabling environment for every member. This recognition that inclusion is not a fixed state, and that we all have responsibility and a role to play in challenging discrimination and oppression, represents an important philosophical shift away from the concept of integration which promoted the sharing of a common space or activity but neglected the need for ideas and institutions to change in order to put children on a more equal footing.

In 2010 the Conservative manifesto promised to 'end the bias towards inclusion' in relation to special educational needs and disability, and this intention has now been ratified as part of coalition policy. Many campaigners and commentators believe that this policy will be damaging and that what has been lacking, even under New Labour, is political will and an understanding of the underlying concepts upon which the vision of an inclusive education system should be built. The Labour government, according to critics, held back from a full programme for inclusion which would involve the transfer of specialist skills and knowledge to mainstream schools. Proponents of an inclusive education system see this transfer of resources as an essential part of the process. Additionally, they argue that mainstream schools should themselves be restructured to increase their capacity to respond to student diversity. Instead a dual system is being maintained and although there are many success stories there are warnings that we are merely perpetuating a two-tier system which segregates those whom the education system regards as challenging or undesirable.

The closure of special schools in particular has been criticised as inhibiting parental choice and giving rise to an increase in exclusion. As proponents of inclusion have long acknowledged, there is a growing body of children with complex health needs and emotional and behavioural difficulties that it is proving difficult to include successfully in mainstream educational settings. In addition the growth of academy settings and free schools which are largely outside local authority control and regulatory systems begs difficult questions, especially about how selective processes might overlook the 'weaker' pupils who for one reason or other another are less likely to achieve their potential through the educational process.

Writers such as Booth et al. (2006) point out that developing inclusion is not just about the process of increasing participation of children but also about decreasing and eliminating any exclusionary pressures. Of great concern are the numbers of exclusions of young children that are recorded in schools and in other early years provision. Children of five and under are excluded from pre-school settings for a number of reason and whilst there are currently no reliable statistics available for exclusions from maintained nursery settings, in 2008 the government released figures that more than 4000 children under five had been excluded from school or nursery in the previous year (Garner 2008).

These figures showed that 4150 children aged five or under had been excluded, 1450 for physical assaults on an adult and 1010 for assaults on children. Twenty toddlers aged two and under were included in the figures. These were often fixed term rather than permanent exclusions. A subsequent report published by the regulatory body Ofsted (2009) looked into the exclusion of children from 60 primary schools and argued that the numbers they found were very small, especially for children in the foundation stage. This lack of consensus concerning pre-school exclusions makes accurate analysis difficult but nevertheless there have been clear trends identified.

A report from the Children's Commissioner Maggie Atkinson (2009) found that pupils with special educational needs (SEN) were eight times more likely to be permanently excluded from schools and that the 18 per cent of pupils with SEN and no statements of SEN were nine times more likely to be excluded. More than two-thirds of all permanently excluded pupils, according to this analysis, are proven to have some form of identified SEN. Ethnicity was also a significant factor in the statistics with, for example, Black Caribbean pupils nearly four times as likely to be permanently excluded. Seventeen per cent of Irish Traveller children and 15 per cent of Roma Traveller children were also excluded.

In 2013 the campaigning charity Contact a Family (2013) flagged up the issue of the illegal exclusion of disabled children. This often took the form of partial exclusion for part of the day because of behaviour or because the school found it hard to cope for other reasons. Some parents in the survey reported that their children had been suspended for practical reasons such as physical difficulty in attending external trips and visits, often because of lack of adult support.

Ofsted (2009) found that schools that had excluded young children often cited behaviour such as biting other children, refusing to follow instructions, kicking or hitting school staff, throwing chairs, climbing over the school fence and running away. In addition, the school sometimes perceived a sexual element to children's behaviour that caused concern. According to this report (p. 8), the reasons why schools responded by excluding pupils were determined by a combination of factors including the following:

- Their philosophy – whether they believed that exclusion was an appropriate response to young children's behaviour.
- Their capacity to respond to challenges – for example, whether they were fully staffed; whether they had a range of provision to support children whose behaviour was challenging; whether staff were well trained.
- The support they received from their local authority and outside agencies, including the timeliness of such support.

Inclusive education has been criticised as grounded in ideology and often impractical. It is observed that much of the literature has a poor evidence base but instead represents the opinions and views of idealistic groups and individuals (Warnock 2005; Leslie and Skidmore 2009). Assessing the educational benefits of inclusive education is a complex task and there is much debate about what constitutes a benefit as well as concerns regarding the use of narrow criteria which focus exclusively on examination and test results. Nevertheless, there is substantial research to indicate that attending a pre-school setting offers significant social and cognitive benefits for a majority of children. The study by Sylva et al. (2004) on the effective provision of pre-school education (EPPE) found that nursery pupils who show early signs of special educational needs dramatically improve their ability simply by being in pre-school. In 2012 a study led by Professor Ian Walker at Lancaster University (Apps et al. 2012) found that children from disadvantaged homes who went to nursery improved their Key Stage 2 and

Key Stage 3 scores on average by 10–11 per cent more than normal. They also gained half a GCSE more.

The current picture is at times confusing and challenging, but as Tilstone et al. (1998: 131) point out: 'Although this [inclusion] means different things in different places there is a universality to the human rights philosophy of inclusion which suggests that the concept is destined to persist rather than represent the latest educational fad or bandwagon'.

This book is written from a children's rights perspective and therefore unapologetically represents a particular view. It argues that in order to address the challenges we face and to minimise all forms of discrimination, it is necessary for us to reaffirm and celebrate the concept of inclusion. In order to promote inclusion successfully we must also locate it within the context of its scope, origins, meaning and true social, political and historical significance. It is only through greater knowledge and understanding that we can achieve the necessary shared vision, understanding and sense of purpose. Without this our progress is likely to be piecemeal and fragile.

Photograph Intro 1 Playing and learning together

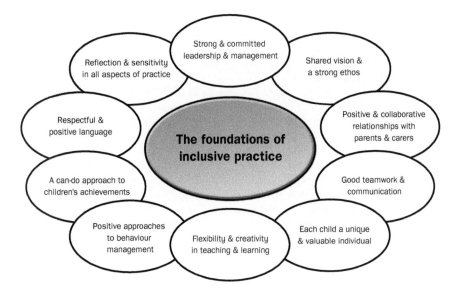

Figure Intro 1   The foundations of inclusive practice

References

Apps, P., Mendola, S. and Walker, I. (2012) *The Impact of Pre-school on Adolescents' Outcomes: Evidence from a Recent English Cohort.* IZA DP No 6971. http://papers.ssrn.com/sol3/papers.cfm?abstract_id=2173661 (accessed 22 May 2013).

Atkinson, M. (2009) *They Never Give Up On You.* www.childrenscommissioner.gov.uk/content/publications/content_562 (accessed 17 April 2013).

Booth, T., Ainscow, M. and Kingston, D. (2006) *Index for Inclusion: Developing Play, Learning and Participation in Early Years and Childcare.* Bristol: Centre for Studies on Inclusive Education.

Contact a Family (2013) *Falling Through the Net.* www.cafamily.org.uk/media/639982/falling_through_the_net_-_illegal_exclusions_report_2013_web.pdf (accessed 17 April 2013).

Department for Education (DfE, 2012a) *The Early Years Foundation Stage.* www.education.gov.uk/schools/teachingandlearning/curriculum/a0068102/early-years-foundation-stage-eyfs (accessed 8 May 2013).

Department for Education (DfE, 2012b) *Support and Aspiration: A New Approach to Special Educational Needs and Disability: Progress and Next Steps.* London: HMSO.

Department for Education and Employment (DfEE, 1997) *Excellence for all Children. Meeting Special Education Needs.* London: HMSO.

Department for Education and Skill (DfES, 2002) *Early Years and the Disability Discrimination Act – What Service Providers Need to Know.* London: National Children's Bureau.

Department for Education and Skill (DfES, 2003) *Every Child Matters.* London: HMSO.

Dickins, M. with Denziloe, J. (2003) *All Together: How to Create Inclusive Services for Disabled Children and their Families. A Practical Handbook for Early Years Workers.* London: National Children's Bureau.

Early Childhood Forum (ECF, 2003) *Policy Statement, Definition of Inclusion* (leaflet). London: National Children's Bureau.

Garner, R. (2008) *More than 4,000 Children under Five Excluded from School.* www.independent.co.uk/news/education/education-news/more-than-4000-children-under-five-excluded-from-school-998193.html (accessed 17 April 2013).

Great Britain Parliament (2001) *Special Educational Needs and Disability Act 2001* (c.2). London: HMSO.

Leslie, C. and Skidmore, C. (2009) *SEN: The Truth about Inclusion.* London: *The Bow Group.*

Nutbrown, C. and Clough, P. (2006) *Inclusion in the Early Years.* London: Sage.

Ofsted (2009) *The Exclusion from School of Children aged Four to Seven.* www.ofsted.gov.uk/resources/exclusion-school-of-children-aged-four-seven (accessed 17 April 2013).

Rustemier, S. (2004) Social justice, in M. Vaughan and G. Thomas (eds). *Inclusive Education – Readings and Reflections.* Maidenhead: Open University Press.

Sylva, K., Melhuish, E., Sammons, P., Siraj-Blatchford, I. and Taggart, B. (2004) *Effective Provision of Pre-school Education (EPPE) Project: Final Report.* London: DfES.

Tilstone, C., Florian, L. and Rose, R. (1998) *Promoting Inclusive Practice.* London: Routledge.

UNICEF (1989) *United Nations Convention on the Rights of the Child.* www.unicef.org/crc/ (accessed 16 March 2013).

Warnock, M. (2005) *Special Educational Needs: A New Look.* London: Philosophy of Education Society of Great Britain.

A

Anti-discriminatory practice
Assessment
Attitude
Autistic spectrum disorder

Anti-discriminatory practice

Anti-discriminatory practice, sometimes known as anti-bias practice, is a proactive approach to working with young children that promotes the valuing of diversity and difference (Brown 1998; Derman-Sparks 1989). Whilst it is primarily concerned with fostering self-esteem, positive individual and group identity and the fulfilment of individual potential, the ultimate goal is to increase the full participation of all groups in wider society.

Anti-discriminatory practice can therefore operate in all areas of the early years experience. Whilst it is derived from the values of families, communities and staff, it is also an approach that embraces a further commitment to social justice and equality in relation to the wider world. An anti-discriminatory approach should be visible in principles, policy and practice. It should entail a collaborative team approach to examining real and/or anticipated problems and issues that may arise that are at odds with the developing inclusive ethos of the setting. The aim is to create a truly welcoming environment that values each individual for who they are and what they bring to the setting.

Anti-discriminatory practice should involve all of the stakeholders in a setting including parents, children and staff. It is about understanding that diversity manifests itself in all of us and that we all have cultural backgrounds and multiple identities derived from a number of sources including our families, our peer groups and our unique set of individual life experiences. Anti-discriminatory practice is also about understanding the connections between the building blocks of identity such as gender, ethnicity, class, ability, sexuality, religion, language/s and any other aspect of discrimination that impact on the child and their family.

At different times in children's lives one or other of these aspects may become a defining feature of the way they view themselves and will mediate how others view them.

Training, resources and materials that support and promote anti-discriminatory practice are most effective when their use or purchase arises from a perceived need that is identified and located within an overall policy and planning process for staff teams, in which everyone has been fully involved. It needs to be recognised that inclusion and equality require a collective learning process for change that includes all staff and stakeholders, including parents and children, so that a common ethos, culture, value system, language and terminology can be established. Through anti-discriminatory practice can come the realisation that we all have internalised layers of expectation based on our upbringing and experiences that operate on a conscious and subconscious level.

Practice example A1

At Tamworth Nursery they have an approach to anti-discriminatory policy-making that involves staff meetings, consulting and observing children and discussion with parents. The policy document is viewed as an active and ongoing document that can change easily through the above mechanisms.

After an incident involving name-calling between children, staff decided that a procedure needed to be set up to deal with such incidents. Staff first talked to the children about their experiences and how such incidents made them feel. This information formed the basis for a meeting involving parents and staff with a view to devising and instigating a clear procedure that was properly understood by all concerned. Some adults were surprised how sensitive and reflective the children's comments were.

For the individual child it is about coming to understand who they are and where they fit into the wider world. Children are not only learning about how they are valued as individuals but also about how their families are regarded and treated. In terms of a child within early education, it is about whether they will be encouraged to grow and extend their interests and abilities or whether they will begin to be shaped and disadvantaged because of the effects of discrimination resulting from the limited and negative expectations of others (Siraj-Blatchford and Clarke 2000; Dickins 2013). Anti-discriminatory practice is a necessary part of the process of becoming inclusive and an essential tool with which to identify and overcome barriers and challenges.

Photograph A1 Enjoying the ride

Assessment

Assessment occurs when we strive to make sense of or give meaning and value to a collection of evidence. For young children evidence may come from general or detailed observations and tests and include information from a range of relevant sources and professionals. The issue of why we should assess young children and how we can do this effectively is of vital importance and the subject of continual debate. As Napier and colleagues (2000: 61) point out, what other people think of us and our abilities matters:

> Our view of ourselves, or self-concept, can therefore be seen to be the product of many different factors: how well we achieve measured by recognised standards of health, wealth or intelligence; how others assess us as based on societal norms of the time; and how we assess ourselves in relation to our own values and beliefs.

The main forms of assessment we see in education are known as formative and summative. *Formative assessment* is the ongoing assessment of children in order to determine teaching and improve learning. *Summative assessment* usually takes the form of a formal process such as the Foundation Stage Profile which is used to assess children's progress and development in terms of set goals and targets. Pollard (2002: 10) compares formative and summative assessment and explores some underlying challenges:

> The basic difference in purpose produces serious tensions between these two forms of assessment – for instance, comparison versus support, product versus process, government versus professional control. Many assessment experts suggest that the effectiveness of one form of assessment is likely to have the unfortunate effect of undermining the effectiveness of the other... In particular when summative testing is emphasised, there is a tendency for teaching to be narrowly directed towards whatever the test measures. A broad and balanced curriculum is thus distorted ... Other commentators feel that the two major forms can be mutually supportive – formative assessment supports the process of learning, summative assessment measures the results.

Formative assessment can be especially problematic for children with learning difficulties and others that differ from expected developmental norms, because a problem in reaching a specific target is often interpreted negatively as 'failure'. On the other hand an achievement that may be significant for an individual child may not be adequately recognised or rewarded as progress because it does not translate into a specific developmental target for the relevant age group.

An approach which limits us to a view of 'ages and stages' is dangerous in that it can lead to adopting a deficit or 'can't do' model of assessing what may be valuable and significant achievements for individual children whose potential in some areas may be limited. Wilson (1998: 44) offers us some insights into these complexities when she refers to 'maturation': the universal sequence which occurs as we age that requires neurological brain development as well as appropriate stimulation in order for functions such as language to develop. There are many reasons why a disabled child might not achieve sufficient physical or intellectual maturation in order to reach developmental goals but as Wilson points out:

> It would be inappropriate, for example, to avoid working towards individual goals in the area most affected by the child's disability on the premise that he or she will never achieve sufficient neurological maturation to accomplish the desired goals anyway. If the goals are important to the child's successful functioning, alternative routes to accomplishing the goals should be identified.
>
> (Wilson 1998: 44)

Whilst acknowledging the importance of what Wilson is saying about avoiding assumptions, this statement highlights the challenge of determining whether or not the goals and targets set for individual children are realistic and achievable.

Practice example A2

Samuel, who is two, was diagnosed with a severe learning disability following an accident which caused brain damage. Although he has physically recovered, his parents were given a poor prognosis of how he might develop intellectually in the future.

Staff at the children's centre that he attends are determined not to set limits for Samuel in terms of what he might achieve. They identify communication skills as a priority and set targets for this, including the use of basic Makaton signs to help him communicate his needs. Six months after this strategy is implemented, much to everyone's surprise, Samuel begins to vocalise and say simple words.

This underlines the importance of a 'can-do' approach in relation to assessment and a recognition that each child is unique in terms of which milestones are reached and when.

The purposes and values of observation and assessment are summarised by Wall (2003: 93) as follows:

- Develop our own understanding of children's current competence levels (to assist with individual planning).
- Reflect on the appropriateness of the provision (tasks securing failure for some children, mismatch of curriculum).
- Inform planning (organisation of room, session).
- Inform others (parents, carers, outside professionals, other staff).
- Assess interactions (adult: child, child: child, adult: adult, child: adult).
- Assess specific events (behaviour, speech and language, physical development, social interaction etc.)
- Assess staff (performance, interactions with children, supporting children with activities etc.)

Assessment can therefore be thought of as evaluative in relation to provision and practice. While summative assessment is used to tell parents, the receiving teacher or other professionals what the child can do and may give examples to support the decision, formative assessment should be used to help children to progress – pinpointing their strengths and finding ways to support learning and development. For disabled children this process can be used to contribute to a diagnosis which indicates whether a child has a developmental delay or disability and for the formal process of assessment before the issue of a statement of special educational need.

An assessment should be an objective process based on collected evidence over a period of time and continuous assessment involves making ongoing assessments of a systematic kind as well as informal judgements from anecdotal records; collecting evidence from a multidisciplinary group of professionals and carers who are involved with the child and recording significant achievements, surprising or unusual reactions, strategies used by the child and evidence of any difficulty or problems.

In some instances it may be necessary to instigate an assessment called the Common Assessment Framework (CAF; DfE 2012). The CAF is a four-step process whereby practitioners can identify a child's or young person's needs early, assess those needs holistically, deliver coordinated services and review progress. The CAF is designed to be used when a practitioner or parent is worried about how well a child or young person is progressing (e.g. concerns about their health, development, welfare, behaviour, progress in learning or any other aspect of their well-being.)

In an inclusive environment it is vital that every child should be recognised, valued and rewarded for any progress in relation to their individual potential for learning and development which in some cases may be limited and constrained by their circumstances, impairment or condition.

Attitude

The issue of attitude is fundamental to any discussion about inclusion. There is no doubt that negative attitudes to difference are the single biggest barrier to successful inclusive education and indeed history has shown that they can underpin and influence social policy on a much wider scale (Rieser and Mason 1992; Vaughan and Thomas 2004). In addition a negative attitude towards individual or groups of children can be damaging in terms of their social and emotional development. Attitude can also positively or negatively influence all outcomes for children.

Siraj-Blatchford and Clarke (2000: 3) argue: 'The way children feel about themselves is not innate or inherited – it is learned'. She cites a body of research (Lawrence 1988; Siraj-Blatchford 1994) that exists to indicate that children's self-esteem can be determined by whether or not they feel that others see them as competent and worthwhile. Roberts (1998) also points out that interactions and relationships are central to the process of the development of self-esteem and identity.

Babies and young children with repeated negative experiences tend to have a reactive stress response as if they are more alert to negative experiences and so produce cortisol more readily. Also their cortisol levels reduce less quickly following a stressful event. This can then have a detrimental effect on synapse development and the neurotransmitters that support positive emotionality, thereby negatively impacting on learning and positive social relationships (Gerhardt 2004).

Although many early years settings strive to be havens of acceptance and belonging, they do not exist in a vacuum but are microcosms that tend to reflect and absorb the views and influences within their local communities and society in general. Young children readily tune in to overt and subtle messages about who is considered better than whom and who is valued in society at a time when they are developing their overall sense of identity and self-worth. Work by Paul Connolly and colleagues (2002) in Northern Ireland as part of the peace and reconciliation process reveals that young children are subjected to a large number of direct and indirect influences including the media, although the main influences are family, local community and school.

Urie Bronfenbrenner (1979) highlighted the notion that the culture of the home, which he termed the microsystem, operates within the context of the wider culture. He defined three additional contextual layers. He writes of the mesosystem which he thinks of as the relationship between two microsystems. For a young child this might be the interrelationship of home and nursery. Bronfenbrenner terms the next layer the exosystem and in this cultural context he includes factors which significantly influence other family members such as places of worship and places of work. Finally, he identifies a macrosystem which includes political, economic, social, legal and educational systems, claiming that these impact on the child since they affect the culture of the home. Using this model it is possible to argue that negative attitudes can permeate through all these layers to the detriment of young children's achievements, aspirations and overall development.

The attitude of practitioners and managers is also crucial. It is important for those who work with families to be aware of their own attitudes and beliefs which can subsequently impact on their relationship with parents and carers and, consequently, on the child's learning and development. For example, Whalley (2004: 85) emphasises the importance of an approach to working with parents in which 'the adult has awareness of the impact of their own attitudes and beliefs and how these might affect the child's learning'. This statement highlights how practitioners' opinions can hinder or strengthen the development of a healthy working relationship, which in turn may be detrimental to certain children's learning and development. The implications are that in order to develop and extend inclusive practice, managers' and practitioners' settings need to consider how these issues may be impacting on the accessibility and quality of their service, especially in terms of the experience of children and families.

Also of concern is how attitude can influence how children feel about each other. Data on primary school children (DCSF 2010) revealed that of over 250,000 six to ten year olds, just under half had been bullied at school and 20 per cent away from school. Among these, two-fifths of those who were bullied at school and one-third of those bullied outside said it occurred on a frequent basis.

The way in which a young child develops an attitude towards difference is likely to be complex and individual. However, Louise Derman-Sparks and colleagues (1980) have argued that not only do young children notice and classify differences, but they also begin to ascribe different values to groups of people according to the responses and behaviour of the adults and children around them. Children as young as two may start asking questions and making comments about differences such as disabilities, gender, physical characteristics (including skin colour), cultural differences and family lifestyles (Derman-Sparks et al. 1980). According to MacNaughton (2006) three year olds can and do recognise physical differences and may develop prejudices around these.

> ### Practice example A3
>
> A four-year-old white girl, Charlotte, on arriving at her playgroup said to one of the workers, Sonia, 'There are bad men outside.' When Sonia went outside to see what she had seen there was a group of Sikh taxi drivers wearing turbans talking together around one of their taxis. When Sonia told her mother what she had said she was shocked and said that neither she nor her father had ever said anything to her like this. Neither were they hostile to Sikh men. As a result of this the workers decided to talk more openly with the children in order to raise the issues involved in this incident and to try to identify the reasons why Charlotte had made the assumptions she had.
>
> (Lane 2008: 163)

Developing and maintaining a positive attitude is not always easy as it will also involve self-scrutiny which may at times be challenging. Access to appropriate training and support, opportunities for honest personal and professional reflection and the celebration and sharing of positive practice are fundamental to the process of attitude change.

Autistic spectrum disorder

Autistic spectrum disorder, usually known as ASD or autism, is a complex disorder with no known cause, but there is evidence to suggest that it can occur due to environmental factors and/or a genetic predisposition. About 60 per 10,000 children under eight have some form of autism (Medical Research Council 2001).

The condition of autism has probably been with us throughout history, although the term was first used by Eugen Bleuler to describe a psychiatric patient who had withdrawn from the world. Research into the condition was pioneered by Hans Asperger and Leo Kanner in the 1940s. Asperger tended to describe children who were more able, whilst Kanner described children who were more severely affected. This distinction is still made today with children at the less severe end of the spectrum commonly referred to as having Asperger's syndrome.

Children with ASDs are affected in a huge variety of ways and to very different degrees, hence the term autistic 'spectrum'. Autism can affect children with any level of intellectual ability, from those who are profoundly learning disabled to those with average or high intelligence. The more seriously affected children at one end of the spectrum have learning difficulties as well and require high levels of support. At the other end of the spectrum, those with Asperger's syndrome or with high-functioning autism are often intelligent academically but they still experience significant social and communication difficulties. Some children have other difficulties which are not directly related to their ASD such as hypermobility, dyspraxia, dyslexia or attention deficit hyperactivity disorder (ADHD).

Children with ASD have significant difficulties relating to other people in a meaningful way. Their ability to develop relationships is impaired, as is their capacity to understand other people's feelings and the social rules of communication. Everyone with an ASD has difficulties in three main areas. This is known as 'the triad of impairments' (Wing and Gould 1979) and they are:

- social understanding and social behaviour
- social communication (verbal and non-verbal)
- rigidity of thinking and difficulties with social imagination.

Although all children with autism have impairments in all three areas however, the ways in which these three impairments manifest themselves vary enormously. A significant number of children with an ASD are either very sensitive (hypersensitive) or under-sensitive (hyposensitive) in one or more of their senses. They may have heightened sensitivity to certain types of sound, touch, texture, taste of food, light, colour or smell. Something like a clothes label, for example, might cause a child extreme discomfort. Other children lack sensory awareness of temperature or pain. Some children shift between hypersensitivity and hyposensitivity. Sensory difficulties can have a significant impact on behaviour and communication. Temple Grandin (2006: 63) is a woman with autism who is also a successful author and animal scientist. She describes some of the auditory problems she experienced as a child:

> When I was little, loud noises were also a problem, often feeling like dentist's drill hitting a nerve. They actually caused pain. I was scared to death of balloons popping, because the sound was like an explosion in my ear. Minor noises that most people can tune out drove me to distraction.

Another aspect of her condition was her extremely sensitive skin:

> Washing my hair and dressing to go to church were two things I hated as a child. A lot of kids hate Sunday clothes and taking baths. But shampooing actually hurt my scalp. It was as if the fingers rubbing my head had thimbles sewn on them. Scratchy petticoats were like sandpaper scraping away at raw nerve endings.

Children with autism will need additional support to develop understanding of the needs, views and feelings of others and to form good relationships with adults and make friends with peers. They may find it difficult to concentrate and maintain attention, and to take turns and share. In addition they may need help to interact effectively with others, to take turns in conversation, to understand jokes and idioms, to make up their own stories and to predict what might happen next in a story. Some children may also need to use augmentative methods of communication, such as visual support materials, for example, gesture, photographs or symbols. In short, children with autism will need support and understanding to help them make sense of the social and wider world and to interact with it effectively.

Practice example A4

Sophie is a four-year-old who has recently joined the nursery and who has been diagnosed as being on the autistic spectrum. Her family moved into the area and she has been difficult to settle and easily distressed. Sophie makes little attempt to verbalise and her play seems obsessive. She is fascinated by water play and is very hard to distract from this. She has little interest in the other children or in group activities and becomes agitated when situation become hectic, especially when she arrives at the setting and when she is collected.

Staff recognise that the water play area is a place of calm and safety for Sophie and use this as the basis for a range of activities. They start to use the Picture Exchange Communication System (PECS) with her so that she can make her needs known more effectively. In addition they set up a visual timetable so that Sophie is aware of the daily routine and knows when home time is coming. These strategies result in Sophie becoming calmer, starting to engage in other activities and beginning to interact with other children more successfully.

Children with ASD are often regarded as one of the most difficult groups to include in mainstream provision, but this is often a question of the degree to which the child is affected. Given patience and understanding, young children on the autistic spectrum can make good progress with the support that can be offered within an effective and flexible mainstream setting. Any autistic child who has had a successful pre-school experience is much more likely to be successfully included in mainstream education when they are older.

References

Bronfenbrenner, U. (1979) *The Ecology of Human Development.* Cambridge, MA: Harvard University Press.

Brown, B. (1998) *Unlearning Discrimination in the Early Years.* Stoke-on-Trent: Trentham Books.

Connoly, P., Smith, A. and Kelly, B. (2002) *Too Young to Notice?* Belfast: Belfast University Press.

Department for Children, Schools and Families (DCSF, 2010) *Tellus4 National Report*. London: DCSF.

Department for Education (DfE, 2012) *Common Assessment Framework*. www.education.gov.uk/childrenandyoungpeople/strategy/integratedworking/caf (accessed 11 May 2013).

Derman-Sparks, L., Tanaka Higa, C. and Sparks, B. (1980) Children, race and racism: how race awareness develops, *Interracial Books for Children Bulletin*, 11: 3–4.

Derman-Sparks, L. (1989) *Anti-Bias Curriculum: Tools for Empowering Young Children*. Washington, DC: National Association for the Education of Young Children.

Dickins, M. (2013) Supporting the well-being of disabled children and their families, in J. Manning-Morton (ed.) *Exploring Well-being in the Early Years*. Maidenhead: Open University Press.

Gerhardt, S. (2004) *Why Love Matters. How Affection Shapes a Baby's Brain*. Hove/New York: Brunner-Routledge.

Grandin, T. (2006) *Thinking in Pictures*. Toronto: Vintage Books.

Lane, J. (2008) *Young Children and Racial Justice*. London: NCB.

Lawrence, D. (1988) *Enhancing Self-Esteem in the Classroom*. London: Paul Chapman.

MacNaughton, G. (2006) *Respect for Diversity: International Overview*. The Hague: Bernard Van Leer Foundation.

Medical Research Council (MRC, 2001) *Review of Autism Research: Epidemiology and Causes*. London: MRC.

Napier, N., Banton, R. and Medforth, N. (2000) Children and assessment, in D. Wyse and A. Hawtin (eds) *Children: A Multiprofessional Perspective*. London: Arnold.

Pollard, A. (2002) *Reflective Teaching*. London: Continuum.

Rieser, R. and Mason, M. (1992) *Disability Equality in the Classroom: A Human Rights Issue*. London: ILEA.

Roberts, R. (1998) Thinking about me and them, in I. Siraj-Blatchford (ed.) *A Curriculum Development Handbook for Early Childhood Educators*. Stoke-on-Trent: Trentham Books.

Roberts, R. (2010) *Well-Being from Birth*. London: Sage.

Siraj-Blatchford, I. (1994) *The Early Years: Laying the Foundation for Racial Equality*. Stoke-on-Trent: Trentham Books.

Siraj-Blatchford, I. and Clarke, P. (2000) *Supporting Identity, Diversity and Language in the Early Years*. Maidenhead: Open University Press.

Vaughan, M. and Thomas, G. (eds) (2004) *Inclusive Education – Readings and Reflections*. Maidenhead: Open University Press.

Wall, K. (2003) *Special Needs and Early Years*. London: Paul Chapman.

Whalley, M. (2004) *Management in Early Childhood Settings*. London: Paul Chapman.

Wing, L. and Gould, J. (1979) Severe impairments of social interaction and associated abnormalities in children: epidemiology and classification, *Journal of Autism and Developmental Disorders*, 9: 11–29.

Wilson, R.A. (1998) *Special Educational Needs in the Early Years*. London: Routledge.

B

Behaviour
Belonging
Bilingualism

Behaviour

Persistent disruptive behaviour is the biggest cause of exclusion even in the early years (Garner 2008), and difficulties around the behaviour of individual children represent the biggest challenge to inclusion. There is now a general recognition that it is important to focus on children in the early years in order to prevent patterns of behaviour becoming harder to change. However, whether individuals perceive certain behaviours negatively or positively is likely to be highly subjective and subject to a number of influences including family values, background, culture and the fact of having once been a child (Drifte 2004).

The term challenging behaviour is often used to describe behaviours which have a negative impact on the child's social or physical surroundings. These behaviours can range from mildly disruptive to behaviour that is likely to cause physical harm to the child themselves or those around them. In some cases behaviour which adults perceive of as challenging may be forming an important function for the child, for example, 'attention seeking' in order to escape environments, situations or activities that the child finds distressing for some reason, or to draw attention to physical discomfort. Some of these may be relatively common behaviours such as taking clothes off or temper tantrums which are only perceived of as particular difficulties if persistent and seen as inappropriate to the child's level of development. Often, these children may be older, larger and more physically difficult to restrain as is the case with some children with learning difficulties.

In order to gain greater understanding and insights into how we can deal effectively with challenging aspects of children's behaviour it is useful to explore how behaviour problems have been conceptualised and managed in the past. This helps us to recognise that our current approaches and understanding are contextualised within particular ways of considering people and their behaviour.

Until the early 1960s the medical and psychodynamic models of understanding of behaviour perceived of as difficult or unusual tended to have dominance. Using these models behaviour problems are regarded as the visible and physical manifestation of unconscious impulses and conflicts, thus implying that the problem lies within the child. This view underpinned the development of psychoeducational approaches aimed at helping teachers and others to accept children as they are and to attempt to understand why they are behaving as they do. Strategies might thus include establishing a trusting relationship, routine and eliminating external stimuli which may be causing disturbance.

Behaviourist theory and approaches have also been hugely influential in terms of how we currently deal with behavioural difficulties. This approach has its roots in the work of the Russian scientist Ivan Pavlov who developed a technique with dogs known as classical conditioning based on punishment and reward which conditioned them to salivate for food at the sound of a bell rather than at the sight of food as would be normal. This eventually led to the idea of a conditioned response which was later extrapolated to children by American psychologists Watson and Skinner to form what is known as the behaviourist approach.

The central thesis of the behaviourist approach is that behaviour is acquired and maintained through learning that can be attributed to positive and negative reinforcement. For example, if we do something and something pleasant happens to us we are more likely to repeat the behaviour. If we do something and something unpleasant happens to us we are then less likely to repeat that behaviour. This means that rather than questioning the context and causes of the behaviour the major focus is on changing the behaviour itself. However, as Papatheodourou (2005: 32) points out, this approach has limitations because it does not take account of the complexity of the human condition: 'Personal variables and genetic endowment are not seen as entities that can make behaviour happen. Instead they are understood in terms of the way environmental events shape them'.

Terms such as behavioural disorders and emotional and behavioural difficulties reflect the underlying principles of the behavioural approach. Strategies used in settings based on rewards and sanctions such as star charts and even everyday praise are all based on behaviourist thinking. Although they can in some instances be highly effective with individual children, they may be flawed inasmuch as children may not be learning why the behaviour is not acceptable at a cognitive level.

Young children are often at a developmental stage in which their cognition is not highly developed enough for them to know what is expected of them. This can be especially true of some children with learning disabilities who may be unaware that their behaviour is negatively impacting on those around them. Cognitive strategies involve adults introducing certain rules to children and helping them to understand which aspects of their behaviour are unacceptable and why. Instructions, guidance, role play and behaviour rehearsal are some of the cognitive techniques that might be found in a classroom context. Cognitive approaches are different from conventional behavioural approaches because they actively encourage children's self-control

Photograph B1   Learning to take turns and share

of their own behaviour as opposed to the external control of behaviour, usually by adults. In practical terms this means that faced with a child who kept snatching toys, for example, the practitioner would focus on listening and encouraging the child to think about why they behave in this way. They would also encourage empathy and want the child to learn what it feels like for other children if their toys are snatched in this way.

There is also the ecosystemic approach (Bronfenbrenner 1979; Pelligrini 1987) from which viewpoint children and their negative or positive behaviour cannot be seen in isolation from their various contexts so that there is no one linear cause but there may be many reasons. Specific behaviours may thus be due to the confusing systems and circumstances in which children find themselves, and the complex and confusing interrelationships between their families, their communities and their early years setting.

The interactionist approach, sometimes known as 'labelling' theory (Becker 1963) also needs to be mentioned in relation to inclusion because it highlights that our judgement about what is 'normal' or 'abnormal' behaviour depends on our own cultural norms and codes of behaviour. Not only can certain behaviours come to be regarded as deviant and negative because they clash with the current group values and sense of order, but those values and expectations may be vastly different from what is expected in the child's home environment. Papatheodorou (2005: 35) highlights the complexities:

> ... The locus of responsibility is placed upon, and raises many issues for, all professionals since their attitudes, sensitivity, tolerance and ability to cope are bound to influence how children are perceived and handled. For example if a child becomes aggressive labelling may only serve to perpetuate that behaviour as it comes to be seen as what is expected from them.

A fundamental part of positive behaviour management is for practitioners and those involved with children to think honestly and deeply about the attitudes, beliefs and emotions towards children which may affect whether they view certain behaviours as challenging and/or socially unacceptable. This necessitates a process of self-scrutiny through which professionals recognise how they may be negatively categorising children who are different from themselves. Abbott (2005: 107) gives this example:

> Black boys are often literally bigger than their white counterparts and may come from a culture which is more physical. Primary schools in particular are almost entirely staffed by women and, while some white women teachers achieve excellent results with Black boys, it would be remarkable if all white women teachers were free from the racial stereotypes that permeate this society about Black men.

Drifte (2004: 23) points out that a negative judgement about a child usually has a negative consequence for them:

> The child we negatively categorised because they came from a different area or background from ourselves may have been unfairly judged as 'typical of somebody from that estate'. The child who constantly challenged our patience probably ended up being side-lined while we worked with a child whom we considered was more worthy of our attention... Occasionally it's *our* reactions and interactions with a child that can be the cause of some of their behavioural difficulties. When this happens we must have sufficient integrity to understand it, and change our approach to the child.

Observation and detailed recording of the nature and incidence of children's particular behaviours are key strategies that usually underpin successful behaviour management. An inclusive approach to behaviour will take into account the child's perspective as well as systemic or organisational factors that might be exacerbating or even creating the circumstances in which an individual child's behaviour becomes a problem.

Practice example B1

Dan is a three-year-old who has been diagnosed as having a 'global delay'. He has learning difficulties, significant hearing loss and some impairment of vision. His parents are very anxious that he should have experience of a mainstream setting while he is young. Staff at the nursery were nervous about looking after Dan but prepared to give it a try.

At a preliminary visit Dan behaved aggressively to two other children, biting and pulling hair. Strong objections were then raised by some parents who believed that Dan's behaviour and the level of physical care required would jeopardise the safety and well-being of their children.

The staff were worried that they would not be able to handle him. Dan's mother insisted that he was not like this at home. Further observation of Dan on two subsequent visits revealed that he was not in fact the aggressor but had been teased and prodded by the other two children and that this was the cause of his uncharacteristic aggressive response.

This example also highlights the importance of not making assumptions about individual children and how doing so can influence our perspectives to the detriment of the progress and outcomes for a child. A reputation established during the early years for difficult behaviour can go on to blight children's progress throughout their educational life.

Photograph B2   Negotiating the territory

Belonging

The need to have a sense of belonging is a fundamental human characteristic and it is also at the heart of what inclusive practice is striving to provide. Belonging implies that everyone in a setting feels and believes that they are truly accepted for themselves and treated equally. The Early Childhood Forum (ECF 2003: 15) sets out what they believe are the implications of belonging and connecting for practice and in particular for children's learning and consider that from birth children should be:

- forming mutually respectful relationships with close and familiar adults and children, through verbal and non-verbal communication (touch, movement, gestures, signs, dialects and languages)
- learning to recognise and accept the needs and rights of familiar adults and children
- learning how to communicate their own needs and rights (within their intimate groups of children and adults)
- sympathising with the needs of other forms of life (plants and animals), treating them with respect and care
- learning how to show respect for the natural and made environments to which they belong (early years setting, home and neighbourhood)
- learning about family history through the sounds, smells, tastes, stories and artefacts which represent continuity and change in their families and cultures
- learning about their membership of groups and the possibility of being, at times, dependent and independent, acquiescent and assertive, of leading and following in peer groups, family and community
- learning about the groups (including ethnic/racial, cultural, linguistic, religious, social) to which familiar adults and children belong
- gradually learning about their membership of groups beyond their immediate surroundings
- building on their first-hand experiences of belonging and connecting, coming to understand more about other people and other communities, past and present.

Practice example B2

One morning Changchang, whose heritage is Chinese, arrives at the pre-school setting with her grandmother Ling. This is the first time this has happened. The staff support Changchang in taking Ling on a tour of the building to show her all her favourite places and activities. Changchang shows her the family display which also has space for information in different languages. She takes her to the home corner where there is a wok, bowls and chopsticks and proceeds to 'cook' her a pretend bowl of noodles. After this the grandmother often brings Changchang to the setting.

The New Zealand Te Whāriki (New Zealand Ministry of Education 1996) approach is one which is seen as promoting a sense of belonging. This is because it promotes respect for children and their learning and actively seeks to value diversity in all its forms. The Reggio Emilia approach, based on the work of the Italian philosopher Loris Magaluzzi, has been widely praised and emulated because of its involvement of the wider community in the educational process and its commitment to developing every child's capacity to learn. However, as Moss (2001) and MacNaughton (2003) point out, although these models are inspiring, a single, defined approach cannot be effective everywhere and in all situations and may not be transposable between different cultures and systems.

It is very important to remember that messages of exclusion can be subtle as well as overt. It is possible to be a full member of a group with full rights and responsibilities but still feel subtly marginalised and excluded by the actions, words or attitudes of others. In such situations we respond as human beings by feeling frightened, lonely, frustrated, anxious and isolated or angry. If children are experiencing such negative emotions it becomes much more difficult for them to learn and develop effectively.

Bilingualism

The term bilingualism is used to describe someone who can speak two languages as opposed to someone who can only speak one language who is monolingual or someone who can speak more than two languages who is regarded as multilingual. In the UK, which is largely monolingual, there is a general lack of understanding of the concept of bilingualism and what it entails (Whitehead 2010). There are as many definitions as there are types of bilingualism but in practical terms it means that children are operating between two or more languages in the course of day-to-day life.

Childhood bilingualism is usually divided into categories of simultaneous and consecutive (Datta 2000). For example, a child who grows up in a family where parents speak different first languages and is enabled to speak both will be regarded as developing simultaneous bilingualism. In this country consecutive bilingualism mostly occurs when a child for whom English is not the first or home language is exposed to it through education and social relationships, when they attend a preschool setting or primary school.

The main misconception about bilingualism is that it is difficult for children to learn two languages at once and that this will lead to linguistic confusion. This is shown to be fallacious by the fact that many people in the world are successful multilingual communicators. Datta (2000: 17) criticises the notion that children's bilingualism might be a barrier to success in education and points out that that it is contrary to international research evidence; she sees the idea of parents being asked to speak English to their children at home as dangerous and counterproductive:

This is not only damaging to parent–child and wider relationships in the community; it reduces the value of family literacies at a variety of levels, such as family anecdotes, stories in home languages, seeing language enacted in many moods (sad, happy, angry) and in different ways – persuasion, recall, instructions, commands, debates. It works against the most important theoretical concept that language and literacy skills are transferable between languages.

There is a substantial body of research to show that children will probably do better if the practitioner is familiar with the children's language and cultural background and can respond appropriately to their needs. The child's home language should be valued rather than denigrated or viewed as having the potential to cause difficulties with learning. There should be extensive use of intonation, gesture, visual support and repetition to make the new language more comprehensible. Those aspects of the child's identity which are associated with their first language and home culture should be positively reinforced and valued by the setting. Last but not least, difficulties with second language acquisition must not be confused with learning disability or special educational need.

Although there will always be individual differences in the ways that children acquire a second language, researchers such as Tabors (1997: 39) suggest that there is a consistent developmental sequence. Tabors explains that there may first be a period of time when children continue to use their home languages in the second language situation. When they discover that the home language does not work in this situation then children often enter a non-verbal period as they collect information about the new language and perhaps spend some time in sound experimentation. Once they are more confident children begin to go public, using individual words and phrases in the new language. They are then able to begin to develop productive use of the second language. These stages are important because knowing the stage that an individual child is at is a prerequisite for providing effective support and encouragement and enabling progress.

Practice example B3

Meena's family were Turkish speakers and had recently arrived in this country when she started at nursery at the age of four. She settled in well and seemed contented apart from the fact that she used only non-verbal communication as a means of making herself understood. She did this very effectively and socialised well and took part in the full range of activities which she clearly enjoyed. At home she communicated verbally in her first language and there was no sign of any specific language or developmental delay. After six months at the nursery Meena came in one morning and started to communicate in English in clear, fully formed coherent sentences. From this day onwards she proved to be a fluent English speaker.

It is really important that bilingual children in the early stages of learning English are not regarded as language delayed. Many children who are in the process of acquiring English as a second language go through a 'silent period' that can be misdiagnosed. During this time children may be effectively rehearsing the language silently to themselves until they have the confidence to 'go public'. This period can last for six months or longer and is not a passive stage but one in which children will be watching, actively listening and exploring their environment to understand new experiences and to develop new meanings. They will be trying to relate previous knowledge to new contexts.

It is important that children should not feel pressurised to speak until they feel confident enough to do so. However, it is essential that adults continue to talk to the children, to pick up their non-verbal responses and other cues in order to support the child's understanding of meaning, and to involve them in activities. These strategies will help children to internalise the language they hear and to develop a sense of the patterns, meanings and range of the language that they are in the process of acquiring.

References

Abbott, D. (2005) Teachers are failing black boys, in B. Richardson (ed.) *Tell it Like It Is – How Our Schools Fail Black Children.* Stoke-on-Trent: Trentham Books.

Becker, H. (1963) *Outsiders. Studies on the Sociology of Deviance.* New York: Free Press.

Bronfenbrenner, U. (1979) *The Ecology of Human Development.* Cambridge, MA: Harvard University Press.

Datta, M. (2000) *Bilinguality and Literacy: Principles and Practice.* London: Continuum.

Drifte, (2004) *Encouraging Positive Behavior in the Early Years.* London: Paul Chapman.

Early Childhood Forum (ECF, 2003) *Quality in Diversity in Early Learning: A Framework for Early Childhood Practitioners.* London: National Children's Bureau.

Garner, R. (2008) *More than 4,000 children under Five Excluded from School.* www.independent.co.uk/news/education/education-news/more-than-4000-children-under-five-excluded-from-school-998193.html (accessed 17 April 2013).

MacNaughton, G. (2003) *Shaping Early Childhood.* Maidenhead: Open University Press.

Moss, P. (2001) The otherness of Reggio, in L. Abbott and C. Nutbrown (eds) *Experiencing Reggio Emilia.* Maidenhead: Open University Press.

New Zealand Ministry of Education, Te Whāriki (1996) *Developmentally Appropriate Programmes in Early Childhood Services.* Wellington: Learning Media.

Papatheodourou, T. (2005) *Behaviour Problems in the Early Years.* London: Routledge Falmer.

Pelligrini, A.D. (1987) *Applied Child Study: A Developmental Approach.* Hillsdale, NJ: Lawrence Erlbaum Associates, Inc.

Tabors, P. (1997) *One Child, Two Languages: A Guide for Preschool Educators of Children Learning English as a Second Language.* Baltimore, MD: Paul Brookes.

Whitehead, M.R. (2010) *Language and Literacy in the Early Years.* London: Sage.

C

Communication
Culture

Communication

Difficulties around communication for individual children are often cited as a major challenge when establishing inclusive practice. There is no doubt that effective communication skills are fundamental to the success of children's learning. Much teaching is delivered verbally and children require communication skills in order to make friends, participate in group activities and to develop higher-level thinking skills. It is through language and communication that human beings benefit from other people's learning and experience and are able to make abstractions in order to consider issues and concepts indirectly. Gopnik et al. (1999: 100) write:

> The development of language is probably linked to the development of our ... distinctive ability to learn about people and things. It allows us to take advantage of all the things that people before us have discovered about the world. We can see so much further than any other species because we stand (proverbially) on the shoulders of our mothers and fathers.

Whilst the exact nature of how human beings acquire language is still a matter of academic debate, we all recognise that communicating with others is fundamental to becoming a social being. The most important resource for children who are learning to communicate is consistency and continuity of care from adults with whom they have been able to build trusting relationships. Where there is mutual awareness and respect there is also more likely to be motivation to interact, communicate and use language.

Most children learn to talk quickly and easily and with very little effort and support other than exposure to the spoken word and a supportive and stimulating learning environment. The term 'speech and language difficulty' covers a wide range of communication 'problems' that some children may face. Speech and/or language difficulties may be the result of a number of emotional or developmental setbacks including impairments but the extent to which they become 'disabling' in the longer term depends very much on the kind of intervention and support that is offered to the child and their family at the start.

In order to develop inclusive practice it is important that we do not allow perceived communication difficulties and barriers to prevent us from enabling children to acquire the skills and confidence that could be crucial to their future fulfilment and independence. Dickins et al. (2004) make the point that regardless of culture and spoken language, verbal communication is only a small part of what makes up communication as a whole. Also crucial to successful communication of any message are body language, gestures, non-verbal cues, tone of voice, inflection and other sounds. Since spoken language is only one of a range of methods that we employ in order to communicate our thoughts, feelings, information and ideas, when faced with a child who has difficulty in communicating verbally we need to remember that to a large extent we are already 'experts' in interpreting and receiving children's non-verbal messages.

Practice example C1

Robina, who is three and a half, seems to have difficulty following spoken instructions and is regarded by some staff as 'disobedient'. The nursery special educational needs coordinator (SENCo) advises staff to break their language down so that it is easier to understand. Staff begin to use short phrases and give one piece of information at a time. In addition they use gestures, objects and pictures to support the understanding of important words. Robina begins to cooperate and take part in the routines of the setting.

Children may experience difficulties and/or delay for a number of complex and often interacting reasons or there may be no clear cause. Possible causes include all forms of hearing impairment, ear infections and specific difficulties in using their oral muscles effectively, for example, if a child has cerebral palsy. Problems during pregnancy or birth can affect children's developing brains and contribute to their speech and language difficulties as part of a wider developmental delay. There are also a number of recognised syndromes or disorders that cause communication difficulties. For some children speech delay may be all or partly due to a physical or learning disability that is hindering their speech development. For example, many children with Down syndrome experience significant delay in learning to talk. Sometimes it is because there has been a lack of stimulation and the support necessary to develop a child's speech, language and communication skills.

As with any disabling condition the impact on families is significant. As part of a study by Glogowska and Campbell (2004), interviews were conducted with the parents of 20 children identified in their pre-school years as having language difficulties. The responses highlighted the fear of isolation, social stigma and what they saw as the 'medicalisation' of their children's early lives.

Children with speech and language difficulties may have difficulty in listening and attending to what other people are saying. They may have difficulty learning and understanding new words and struggle to put them together in sentences. Speech may be unclear and there may be stammering or other forms of speech impediment. Children with these difficulties will need support to take part in conversation and express their needs effectively.

Photograph C1 Supporting language development with action rhymes and songs

Below are a few principles of good practice when speaking to children with speech and language difficulties and indeed any child who is learning to communicate through speech:

- Attract the child's attention by gently touching them (unless the child objects to this) and saying their name first.
- Make sure the child can see your face when you are speaking.
- Use eye contact.

- Don't turn your face away until you have finished speaking.
- Give instructions in small, understandable 'bite size' amounts.
- Make your language direct and simple.
- Establish a positive and mutually supportive relationship with parents and carers and get as much information from them as you can about how the child already communicates.
- Learn to use any equipment, communication systems or other special facilities that an individual child may have.
- Use pictures, objects and/or symbols to give reinforcement to the spoken word and to support understanding.
- Take your time and be as relaxed and warm as possible.

Case study C2

Jubilee Primary School is an amalgamation of two primary schools and a special school for children with hearing impairments. They have evolved many successful inclusive strategies through training and regular inclusion meetings. All children and staff in the school have signing lessons (British Sign Language, BSL) and it is viewed as an important skill which gives added value to the curriculum at Jubilee school. Total Communication – a system which stresses the importance of using all possible communication methods equally – is used. So, for instance, sign language is combined with lip-reading as well as traditional methods of listening and encouraging emergent language skills. Parents can go to an after-school club with their children to learn signing. The aim is to create a fully signing school.

To a great extent communicating with young children, particularly if their needs are complex, means acknowledging and fine tuning the non-verbal communication skills we already use every day (Triangle 2001). In some cases additional techniques may be necessary and listed below are some of the most common:

1. **Braille** is a method of reading by touch used by people with visual impairments, usually written on a machine called a Brailler, which is like a typewriter but only has six keys. The Royal National Institute for Blind People (RNIB) runs a translation service.
2. **British Sign Language (BSL)** is the sign language used by the deaf community in Britain. It has a structure and grammar that is different to English and cannot be used at the same time as spoken English.
3. **Blissymbols** were developed as an alternative means of communication for children with cerebral palsy. A child using Bliss will have their own board or chart with a range of symbols appropriate to their needs. They may indicate

the symbols they wish to use in a variety of ways, such as pointing or eye movements.

4. **Cued speech** is used alongside lip-reading to help children understand what they are seeing on the lips. The system has a series of hand shapes to represent consonants and positions around or near the mouth that can be touched to represent vowels. The system is particularly useful in helping children distinguish words that look very similar when they are lip-reading.

5. **Deafblind Manual Alphabet** is designed for people who are deaf and blind, and whose understanding can only be reached through the sense of touch. This is achieved by a speaker pressing their hand firmly on the hand of the deafblind person using the various signs of this alphabet.

6. **Electronic communication** – speech synthesisers and digitised speech machines linked to computers are examples of the way in which micro-technology can aid communication. While there is no automatic enti-tlement to these devices on the NHS, there is a national network of communication aids centres, usually attached to hospitals, which will make free assessments.

7. **Lip-reading** is the ability to read the patterns that people make with their lips when they speak.

8. **Makaton** uses signs (gestures) and symbols (pictures) depicting selected concepts to help hearing people who have learning and communication difficulties. There is a core vocabulary of 450 signs and symbols, each repre-senting a basic concept, which can be further supported by signs and sym-bols representing up to 7000 other concepts. Makaton is an aid to commu-nication, not a language in itself. Signs and symbols are derived from BSL, used in the order they would be spoken in English, and are accompanied by spoken English.

9. **Moon** is a system of reading by touch by using raised shapes. It is more com-monly used by blind or partially sighted adults or children who find Braille too difficult to feel or learn. It uses shapes that are more like the written word.

10. **Paget Gorman signed speech** is a sign system which is used at the same time as spoken language to make clear the structure of the English language. Its primary function is educational: to develop an understanding of the use of language and to give access to written and spoken English. It is used mainly with children who have specific speech and language disorders.

11. **Picture Exchange Communication System (PECS)** is an approach that teaches early communication skills using pictures rather than words or sign-ing. With PECS children are taught to exchange pictures for something they want. This exchange format incorporates skills such as social approach and interacting with another person.

12. **Signed English** consists of signs taken from BSL, together with specially developed signs which are only used in Signed English. It is designed to be used at the same time as spoken English rather than separately from it.

13. **Signalong** is a sign vocabulary also based on BSL, designed to help children and adults with learning difficulties to acquire language skills and to aid where there are communication difficulties. The extensive vocabulary of signs is always used with speech and therefore used in English word order. Signalong is intended for use in environments in which spoken language is the main form of communication.

14. **Total communication** is a way of approaching communication with children which stresses the importance of using all possible communication methods equally if a child with hearing loss is to gain an understanding of language – so, for instance, sign language would be combined with lip-reading.

Inclusive strategies will often involve all of the children in the group learning simple signing systems such as Makaton or Signalong so that the child who is experiencing difficulties does not feel isolated or stigmatised. For more information on communication and speech and language difficulties see these links: http://foundationyears.org.uk/wp-content/uploads/2011/10/Inclusion_Development_Programme_Speech_Language+Communication.pdf.

www.ican.org.uk/.

Culture

Everyone has a culture as a result of their lives and experiences. It is generally understood that elements of culture may include factors such as language, social class, religious beliefs and practices, traditions, dress and food. However, this understanding can be problematic, as Lane (2008: 80) describes:

> The word 'culture' is often only used to describe the culture of people who are black...Cultural stereotyping is not only ridiculous, it is dangerous, because it makes assumptions that do not reflect reality. Everyone has a culture, or cultures, but it seems that only *some* people are required to define what their culture means for them. Most white English people just take whatever their culture is for granted and find it difficult to define in precise terms, whereas other white British people – the Welsh, Scottish, Irish – can clearly talk about their own distinctive cultures

Lane is making a very important point about the danger of making assumptions with little or no information about the individual child or family culture. It is also clear that the notion of a defined culture as such is more important for some than for others. This does not mean that early years providers should not become culturally aware. Indeed, knowledge of and respect for conventions, customs, communication and belief and value systems are intrinsic to the inclusive approach and to establishing positive relationships with children and families.

Photograph C2   Learning about each other

Pence and Nsamenang (2008: 18) talk about cultural identity as the: 'feeling of "belonging" together experienced by a group of people'. For example, language and dialect or accent are important ways in which human beings distinguish themselves from one another. For children, acquisition of a cultural identity starts with early family experiences but as they grow community begins to play an increasingly important role.

In the public mind some groups or 'cultures' are seen as less likely to be successful in academic terms. Siraj-Blatchford and Clarke (2000: 7) express concern about the effects of such cultural stereotyping on young children in terms of the identity that they construct:

> It is apparent that certain confounding identities, for instance, white/working/class/male, can lead to lower outcomes because of expectations held by the children and adults. In asserting their masculinity, white, working-class boys might choose gross-motor construction activities over reading and pre-reading activities.

Most early years settings currently have a multicultural approach to these issues. However, it is generally recognised that multiculturalism on its own may simply provide ammunition to reinforce racism unless there is recognition of the way that different cultures are ranked in a racial hierarchy (Lane 2008).

Practice example C3

At Mulberry Children's Centre staff make a point of greeting parents and children in their first language. Many parents comment on how this practice contributes to their feeling welcome in the setting. Staff decide to invite parents to tell stories to the children in different languages. All are surprised at how much the children enjoy these sessions even though they do not, in most cases, understand a word.

Multiculturalism is therefore a hotly debated topic and there are continual disagreements and discussions about what it is and whether or not it is a good thing for society. In the context of anti-discriminatory practice it is essential that we recognise the existence of other cultures; the right of the individual to speak their language and practise their culture and religion; and the need for these practices to be acknowledged and valued in our settings and in wider society. Because everyone has a culture, multiculturalism should be about all of us being open to the influence of others and to value the gifts and insights they can bring to us. Lane (2008: 143) points out:

> The fact remains that we all live in a multicultural society. Whether all the component cultures are equal, whether they are encouraged to be separate, whether cultures see themselves as separate, whether racial discrimination is removed and what are the consequent implications for our society is the crux of the discussion.

Whilst the debate continues, it is clear within the current context that group and individual culture needs to be valued and respected as part of a child's individual identity. Although the nature and relative success of multiculturalism in society remains a matter of debate and opinion, this aspect of practice is non-negotiable in an inclusive setting.

References

Dickins, M., Emerson, S. and Gordon-Smith, P. (2004) *Starting with Choice: Inclusive Strategies for Consulting Young Children.* London: Save the Children.

Glogowska, M. and Campbell, R. (2004) Parental views of surveillance for early speech and language difficulties, *Children and Society*, 18(4): 266–277.

Gopnik, A., Meltzoff, A. and Kuhl, P. (1999) *How Babies Think.* London: Weidenfeld & Nicolson.

Lane, J. (2008) *Young Children and Racial Justice.* London: National Children's Bureau.

Pence, A. and Nsamenang, B. (2008) A case for early childhood development, in L. Brooker and M. Woodhead. *Early Childhood in Focus 3 Diversity and Young Children: Developing Positive Identities.* Maidenhead: Open University Press.

Siraj-Blatchford, I. and Clarke, P. (2000) *Supporting Identity, Diversity and Language in the Early Years.* Maidenhead: Open University Press.

Triangle (2001) *Two-Way Street: Communication Handbook.* London: NSPCC.

D

Developmental perspectives
Difficulties with learning
Disability
Diversity

Developmental perspectives

A developmental perspective is an approach that usually locates the child within a prescribed framework of 'stages' and levels of attainment. Taking a developmental perspective means the acquisition of knowledge and understanding about developmental patterns for children's physical growth as well as for cognitive, social and emotional, and language aspects of development. This approach can be very useful but also problematic because, as Wilson (1998: 44) points out:

> Development is far more complex than age. Age marks the passage of time – i.e. how much time has elapsed since the child's birth or, when talking about prenatal development, how much time has elapsed since conception. Development, however, occurs when the complexity of a child's behaviour increases.

Wilson also makes an important distinction between maturation and development, describing maturation as a universal sequence of biological changes that occur as children grow. Maturation is a prerequisite for certain aspects of development as in language development, for example. Before a child can develop the capability and capacity to understand and produce language, the brain must first develop sufficiently for this to happen. Difficulties and misunderstandings can occur when maturation is delayed, for example, if a child has brain damage. Wilson (1998: 44) explains:

> It would be inappropriate, for example, to avoid working towards individual goals in the area most affected by the child's disability on the premise that

he or she will never achieve sufficient neurological maturation to accomplish the desired goals anyway. If the goals are important to the child's successful functioning, alternative routes to accomplishing the goals should be identified. In the case of a child with severe brain damage who may be prevented forever from developing a broad repertoire of language skills, the goal of successful communication must still be pursued.

In writing about child development Robert Myers (1991) refers to the changes which occur as children make quantitative shifts towards more complex movement, thought and interpersonal relationships. Myers outlines a number of vital factors and points out that all aspects of development are interrelated. For example, when children are hungry they do not learn as well as when they are well nourished; when children are insecure they do not learn as well as children who have a secure attachment to another person. Importantly, just as adverse conditions can disrupt aspects of development, so improved conditions can also enhance it. Development is therefore not just a passive process, but occurs through active interaction and engagement with people, objects and situations. Although there are some common features of development, each child's development is totally unique.

In the United States there has been a move to what has been termed Developmentally Appropriate Practice (DAP) which has influenced practice in other countries as well. This approach recognises the importance of child development, while seeking to ensure that the curriculum itself and the means of delivery take account of children's individual strengths, needs and interests. Nutbrown et al. (2006: 12) set out 12 key principles:

1. Domains of children's development – physical, social, emotional and cognitive – are closely related. Development in one domain influences and is influenced by development in other domains.
2. Development occurs in a relatively orderly sequence, with later abilities, skills and knowledge building on those already acquired.
3. Development proceeds at varying rates from child to child as well as unevenly within different areas of each child's functioning.
4. Early experiences have both cumulative and delayed effects on individual children's development; optimal periods exist for certain types of development and learning.
5. Development proceeds in predictable directions towards greater complexity, organisation and internalisation.
6. Development and learning occur in and are influenced by multiple social and cultural contexts.
7. Children are active learners, drawing on direct physical and social experience as well as culturally transmitted knowledge to construct their own understanding of the world around them.

8. Development and learning result from interaction of biological maturation and the environment, which includes the physical and social worlds that children live in.
9. Play is an important vehicle for children's social, emotional and cognitive development, as well as a reflection of their development.
10. Development advances when children have opportunities to practise newly acquired skills as well as when they experience a challenge just beyond the level of their present mastery.
11. Children demonstrate different modes of knowing and learning and different ways of representing what they know.
12. Children develop and learn best in the context of a community where they are safe and valued, their physical needs are met, and they feel psychologically secure.

Guidelines for developmentally appropriate practice focus on curriculum, adult and child interaction, relations between home and early years setting, and assessment, including the developmental evaluation of children. Each area of focus is followed by a number of statements of principle, supported by references to theory, for practitioners to follow up ideas in greater detail.

Since the publication by Bredekamp and Copple (1997) of *Developmentally Appropriate Practice in Early Childhood Programs*, writers such as Erica Burman have been highly critical of the concept of 'developmentalism' and 'developmental psychology' which Burman (1994: 9) identifies as the driving force behind developmentalism, saying it: 'has been driven by the demand to produce technologies of measurement'. For Burman and others, one result has been unhelpful pressure on mothers by highlighting children's needs and the requirement to do what is 'best' for them' (Burman 1994: 3-4). According to Burman, this emphasis has contributed to the ongoing subjection of women within society and is also being used 'to classify and stratify individuals, groups and populations so as to maintain class, gender and racial oppression'.

For its critics, developmental psychology is seen as generally taking insufficient account of the context and environment in which children learn and develop. Martin Woodhead (1998) also has reservations about universal measurements of quality. He argues that DAP is based on the assumption of a universal sequence of development and change. He criticises DAP on the basis that it needs to be more contextually situated and culturally relevant. Woodhead cites a typical situation in Kenya where there may be one teacher to 60 children.

Wilson (1998) does recommend individualised objectives for children based on a developmental approach to the curriculum. However, she believes that the criteria for objectives which reflect DAP should be broadly written and allow for flexibility. For Wilson effective targets are those which allow for implementation in the daily routine, serve a functional purpose and reflect competence as well as concerns. All too often targets are set for children which do not engage with the underlying social and emotional issues that may be impeding learning in the first place.

What is really important here is that in our pursuit of developmental frameworks to apply, we do not adopt a deficit model of individual children's achievements and consequently label them as failures if they do not succeed in reaching prescribed targets and developmental goals. Any targets we set should be appropriate, logical, individual and achievable so that every child is enabled to experience success and be motivated by it.

Difficulties with learning

When a child continues to struggle with specific aspects of learning this may sometimes be due to a learning disability. The needs and requirements of children with a learning disability are often misunderstood and learning disability itself is often confused in the public mind with mental health disorders and conditions. Many in the field believe that a distinction also needs to be made between specific learning difficulties such as dyslexia and that the definition of learning disabilities needs to focus on those who have difficulty learning across more than one area of their lives and not just reading and writing. Learning disability can be all or part of an enormous number and range of conditions of which the most common are Down syndrome, autistic spectrum disorder and cerebral palsy.

A child with a learning disability will usually have a reduced intellectual capacity and ability to deal with everyday activities and these challenges are likely to be lifelong. In practical terms this means that it is harder for a child to learn, understand and communicate than it is for other children. They may find it difficult, for example, to understand new or complex information and have difficulty learning new skills and coping independently.

Although sometimes there is no known cause for a particular learning disability several factors can affect brain development in this way, including the mother's illness in pregnancy, any problems at birth which prevent oxygen getting to the brain, genetically inherited conditions and illness such as meningitis or injury in early childhood.

Practice example D1

Sofia, who is three, has a moderate learning disability and has been slow to socialise effectively with the other children. A series of observations reveal that although she is well liked by the other children and staff she is often treated as a 'pet' and her independence is not being sufficiently encouraged.

An individual education plan is drawn up that reflects this concern and Sofia is encouraged to take responsibility for tasks such as hanging up her own coat on the right peg and going to the toilet independently. As Sofia increases in confidence she becomes more assertive in her relationships with others and begins to interact with them as equals.

When working with children with learning disabilities the aim is to build on their existing strengths and establish the conditions in which the individual child learns best. The needs and entitlements of a child with a learning disability are therefore the same as for any child. However, meeting them may entail flexibility and creativity. Setting achievable and appropriate goals and targets is important, as is a commitment to supporting the child to reach their full potential.

Photograph D1   Enjoying the company

Disability

Disability is defined by the Equality Act 2010 as follows: 'A person is disabled if they have a physical or mental impairment which has substantial and long-term adverse effect on a person's ability to perform normal day-to-day activities'

(Great Britain Parliament 2010). This definition includes a wide range of impairments, including hidden impairments. An estimated 770,000 children from 0 to 16 have a disability or longstanding medical condition using this definition. There is also a changing population of disabled children, especially as improved neonatal care has meant the survival of very low birth weight babies or young children with very complex health needs and the associated growth of dependence on technology (Carpenter and Egerton 2005).

Almost all of us will have some life experience of disability at some point. As Dickins with Denziloe (2003: 5) point out this is because:

> disability is a range of difficulties on a continuum that spans minor impairments, such as long-sightedness in middle age, through to profound and multiple disabilities that have a major impact on quality of life. Viewed in this way it becomes clear that disability is a feature of ordinary life that will touch us all at some point, directly or indirectly.

Importantly, and especially in terms of policy, practice and provision, whom we count as disabled will depend on where we draw the line on this vast continuum. Despite this commonality of human experience, many people are still afraid of disability and disabled adults and children are often stigmatised, avoided, patronised or excluded. One issue is that disability is often confused with illness, chronic disease and mental disorders and this helps to create the prejudice and negative attitudes that many disabled people experience.

There are three main models or ways of understanding disability and its impact on disabled people (Rieser and Mason 1992). The moral or religious model of disability is the idea that disability is a punishment for evil behaviour. Societies in which this model is prevalent are much more likely to feel that disabled people and their families should be stigmatised and avoided. Although this idea might have had its genesis in some religious texts, in no way is it meant to imply that all or any religious people will necessarily feel this way. In some countries conditions such as epilepsy are seen as positive and linked to religious hallucinatory experiences but the negative view is much more frequently found.

The medical model of disability is usually described as an attitude of mind that dictates that because disability is caused by an impairment or condition the role of the professionals involved is to cure or alleviate it. Once again this model applies to all of us and not just the medical profession. Viewed from this perspective disability becomes a medical 'problem' which we must 'treat' (UPIAS 1976; Rieser and Mason 1992; Oliver 2004). Dickins with Denziloe (2003: 6) state:

> While there is nothing wrong at all with alleviating suffering or discomfort, the main problem with this model is that impairments are the sole focus of attention. The child becomes a set of problems rather than an individual with strengths and weaknesses to be welcomed into the world with joy and anticipation.

So whilst at face value there may seem nothing untoward about this approach we need to consider the possible subsequent effect on self-esteem and quality of life for some individuals. Runswick-Cole (2008: 176) states:

> A medical model framework emerges from models used in medicine in which practitioners think in terms of 'conditions', 'treatment', 'cure' and 'rehabilitation'. A medical model assumes that the disabled adult or child is deficient but, it is hoped, alterable; whereas society is fixed, with limited capacity for, or willingness to change.

The possibility of a quick remedial solution for disabled children and those with other forms of special educational needs (SEN) is attractive in practical, political and

Figure D1 Medical model thinking

economic terms. However, we need also to remember that many disabilities are life-long and cannot be cured (Dickins 2013) and for these children the approach needs to have a different emphasis. If the child is primarily viewed as 'faulty' they may also be regarded as a 'failure' if various treatment and interventions do not 'cure' the problem. In an inclusive setting children with disabling conditions will be celebrated and accepted *as they are* and practitioners will encourage self-acceptance and a positive self-image and identity in them. Figure D1 shows the effects of medical model thinking.

The social model of disability is intrinsic to the inclusive approach. In this model the 'problem' is located outside the province of disabled children and their families and it is the physical and social barriers that society creates which are regarded as the disabling factors (UPIAS 1976; Rieser and Mason 1992; Oliver 2004). Figure D2 shows the social model of disability.

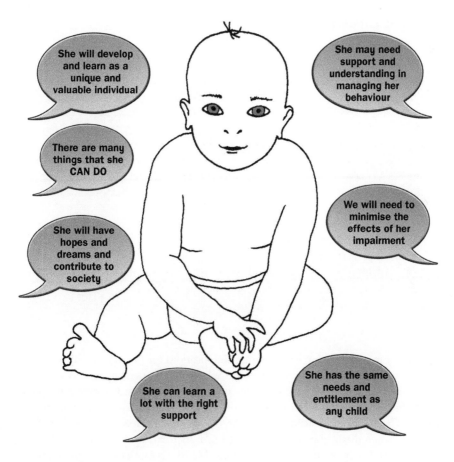

Figure D2   Social model thinking

Read et al. (2012: 224) highlight the influence of the social model:

> The approach makes a distinction between impairment and disability with the latter increasingly being seen as the product of the complex interaction between individual characteristics, including impairment and chronic illness, and the social and cultural context. When disability is understood in this way, the social circumstances of disabled children and their families – always a crucial matter – take on an even greater significance as they are seen to play a major role in producing or reducing disability.

Practice example D2

Robert is four and has previously been diagnosed with mild cerebral palsy which is a neurological condition that affects muscle coordination and movement. He is able to walk and move about without much difficulty but sometimes his speech is unclear. Robert is a bright boy who enjoys learning and socialising with his friends. The setting special educational needs coordinator (SENCo) is concerned that he is still in nappies and instigates a toilet training regime through his individual education plan even though his mother has expressed concern that his condition may make this strategy inappropriate as she has not been able to achieve this at home. The staff feel that ensuring continence will vastly improve his chances of success at the mainstream school he will be attending later in the year.

Despite the well-meaning efforts of the staff, however, Robert remains in nappies as his condition means that he has not developed sufficient muscular control. The staff accept that this may be a lifelong rather than transient aspect of his disability and concentrate their efforts on smoothing his transition to school through effective communication and arranging visits.

Social model thinking has important implications for the way in which we care for and educate children because it is the only model that encourages us to accept and value children whatever their differences. Prejudice towards disabled people is not innate but rather learned through contact with the prejudice and ignorance of others. The notion of inclusion is based on the idea that we will ultimately benefit as a society when disabled people are enabled to fully participate and contribute. The social model has been adopted by the World Health Organization and now underpins much of current thinking and developments.

Photograph D2 Supporting learning through trust

Diversity

Although the term diversity essentially means difference, when used in the context of equality it is usually understood to be about recognising and valuing individual as well as group differences. This means treating people as individuals, and displaying a positive attitude towards all of the differences found in the community and in the workplace. Waller (2005: 118) reminds us:

> Within staff teams, there will be diversity in personality, attitudes, backgrounds, gender, faith and religious beliefs, culture, language and abilities. The starting point, therefore, for professionals will be to acknowledge the differences that exist among colleagues and to treat everyone with respect.

Although the term diversity is usually used in a positive way it is somewhat of a catch-all, and when used in policy and guidance not in itself very helpful. Lane (2008: 81) points out:

> Unless it is explicit that identifying all the aspects of this diversity and ensuring that all the diverse parts are treated equally, or equality is implicit within the

context of the text, then in a society where many people are treated unequally it merely becomes a palliative for changing nothing and continuing as before.

Negative messages about characteristics, attributes, customs or behaviours are often internalised by young children who are in the process of constructing their identities and trying to make sense of what they see and hear around them. Some of these negative messages may be overt but others may be subtle and/or unintentional. It is very likely that any negative behaviour and attitudes the children display will have been learned previously from the reactions of older children, adults or the media. Since children may experience negative responses and attitudes for a wide variety of reasons, sensitive observation and proactive anti-discriminatory approaches need to be embedded in everyday policy and practice.

References

Bredekamp, S. and Copple, C. (eds) (1997) *Developmentally Appropriate Practice in Early Childhood Programs*. Washington, DC: NAEYC.

Burman, E. (1994) *Deconstructing Developmental Psychology*. New York: Routledge.

Carpenter, B. and Egerton, J. (2005) *Early Childhood Intervention – International Perspectives*. Coventry: National Initiatives and Regional Practice, West Midlands SEN Regional Partnership.

Dickins, M. with Denziloe, J. (2003) *All Together: How to Create Inclusive Services for Disabled Children and their Families*. London: National Children's Bureau.

Dickins, M. (2013) Supporting the well-being of disabled children and their families, in J. Manning-Morton (ed.) *Exploring Well-being in Early Childhood*. Maidenhead: Open University Press.

Great Britain Parliament (2010) *Equality Act 2010*. London: HMSO.

Lane, J. (2008) *Young Children and Racial Justice*. London: National Children's Bureau.

Myers, R. (1991) *Towards a Fair Start for Children*. Paris: UNESCO.

Nutbrown, C., Clough, P. and Atherton, F. (eds) (2006) *Inclusion in the Early Years*. London: Sage.

Oliver, M. (2004) The social model in action, in C. Barnes and G. Mercer (eds) *Implementing the Social Model of Disability: Theory and Research*. Leeds: Disability Press.

Read, J., Blackburn, C. and Spencer, C. (2012) Disabled children and their families: a decade of policy change, *Children and Society*, 26: 223–233.

Rieser, R. and Mason, M. (1992) *Disability Equality in the Classroom: A Human Rights Issue*. London: ILEA.

Runswick-Cole, K. (2008) Between a rock and a hard place: parents' attitudes to the inclusion of children with special educational needs in mainstream and special schools, *British Journal of Special Education*, 35(3): 173–180.

Union of the Physically Impaired Against Segregation (UPIAS, 1976) *Fundamental Principles of Disability*. London: UPIAS.

Waller, T. (ed.) (2005) *An Introduction to Early Childhood*. London: Sage.

Wilson, R. (1998) *Special Educational Needs in the Early Years*. London: Routledge.

Woodhead, M. (1998) 'Quality' in early childhood programmes – a contextually appropriate approach, *International Journal of Early Childhood*, 6(1): 5–18.

E

Early intervention

One of the challenges for any discussion of early intervention is the lack of a statutory or commonly understood definition as this means that the term is often used in a variety of ways. Although, historically, early intervention has been regarded as a service targeting individual children, from the 1970s onwards there has been an increasing emphasis on the importance of parents and a subsequent recognition that high-quality family support is an essential element within any early intervention programme. So although early intervention was once regarded as in the domain of special educational needs (SEN) and disability, understanding of the term is often widened to include social exclusion and almost every strategy we employ with children and families. For example, Sylva et al. (2004) have recently broadened the definition to include high-quality, generic early years education and childcare.

Early intervention in its broadest sense can happen at any time in a child's life, but here the term is being used to describe services and approaches that come into play when children are young. This exploration of early intervention will also make a distinction between *individual* early support for those children with continuing, possibly deteriorating conditions, and those *family* interventions which are aimed at reducing the impact of factors putting children at risk, either in the context of child protection or those where SEN may be pre-empted, such as those children at risk of social exclusion as a result of emotional and social behavioural difficulties. The goals of any particular early intervention strategy may therefore be as wide as decreasing poverty and inequality or as narrow as a behaviour strategy targeting an individual child.

In recent years it has been widely recognised that early family interventions have the potential to improve outcomes for children. Far more is known now about the extent to which a child's early development, including before birth, lays the foundation for their future life. A report by the children's organisation C4EO which looked at UK and international evidence states:

> The most striking message is that early intervention clearly works – when it is an appropriate intervention, applied well, following timely identification of a problem; and the earlier the better to secure maximum impact and greatest long term sustainability (both as early in the child's life as possible and/or as soon as possible after a difficulty becomes apparent). The wealth of effective local, national and international practice showing evidence of improvements in outcomes and the quality of life for many children and families gives cause for optimism, and encouragement to replicate local innovations more widely. Indeed, some of the examples describe practice that has already spread widely (often internationally) from its local origins.
>
> (C4EO 2010:4)

Despite this optimistic consensus about the possibilities, there is currently no coherent and consistent policy approach as to how, when, where or to whom strategies should be delivered. Policy in the UK is currently centred on targeting those families and children deemed to be dysfunctional, disadvantaged and at risk of family breakdown and/or school failure. In a recent report (Allen 2011) early intervention is described as having the capacity to break intergenerational cycles of dysfunction and underachievement so that destructive patterns of behaviour are not passed on.

However, Allen (2011: 3) goes on to state that the prime objective should be to produce high levels of 'school readiness' for all children regardless of family income. This approach is seen as contentious in that the focus on school readiness fails to take into account that children in the UK start school earlier than in many other countries. It also appears to represent a linear strategy rather than a holistic approach to child well-being and development. It neglects the role that wider factors such as unemployment, poverty and lack of housing may be playing, choosing instead to focus on the perceived shortcomings of individual families (Dickins 2013). An inclusive approach to this issue would clearly put the emphasis on schools being ready for individual children rather than the reverse.

There is an ongoing debate about how to determine the best value of different approaches to early intervention and education. *The Effective Provision of Pre-school Education* (EPPE, Sylva et al. 2004) collected a wide range of information on over 3000 children, their parents, their home environments and the wide range of pre-school settings which they attended. A key question within the EPPE study is whether some early intervention/pre-school settings are more effective than others. The EPPE study concluded that supporting children's home learning is crucial and that disadvantaged children do best in mixed social groups rather than in settings with other disadvantaged children. They also found that the type of pre-school experience has an important part in children's develop-mental progress and that integrated centres (i.e. those combining education and care) tend to promote better social development, regardless of background and prior social behaviour.

In terms of good practice there are common features of both individual and family interventions. Sheila Wolfendale (2000: 4), in an analysis of different UK approaches, states that early intervention typically has four primary goals:

1. To sustain families in supporting their children's development.
2. To promote children's development in key domains (e.g. cognitive, social, physical, emotional, linguistic) through the early years curriculum and other learning opportunities.
3. To promote children's confidence and coping skills.
4. To prevent the emergence of future problems.

Seen from this perspective, appropriate 'early intervention' describes many of the processes and strategies that already take place in an effective early years settings.

Case study E1

Early Support is a funded programme, which was set up to improve the delivery of services for families of children with disabilities aged 0–3 years in England at a national, regional and local level. It began as a pilot programme based on the Sure Start initiative and was developed in response to the UK government guidance *Together from the Start* (DfES 2003a). Its remit was to take forward the principles within that guidance.

Since Early Support was established, it has influenced many government policy documents including *Every Child Matters* (DfES 2003b). The role of individual Early Support programmes is to raise expectations about the way agencies and services work, and to provide encouragement for change, as well as providing practical tools and training to support multi-agency service develop-ment at a local level.

The most obvious reason for early intervention for individual children is that the earlier a child's needs are addressed, then the more progress the child is likely to make. Evidence suggests that there are several neurobiological and behavioural mechanisms that create unique opportunities in the early years to enhance chil-dren's overall development and prevent some problems from emerging (Seigal 1999; Goddard Blythe 2008). However, ensuring that interventions are appropri-ate to the overall needs and entitlements of individual children raises complex and thought provoking questions that lie at the heart of early years care and education. Dickins with Denziloe (2003: 7) point out:

> We need to ensure that any intervention we undertake for children in our settings is truly enabling and not destructive to the development of a positive identity and self-image. We need to question a focus that has its primary roots in the medical model, and temper our zeal for a 'quick fix' solution to children's 'problems' by listening more carefully to the voices of disabled adults and older children who have experienced some interventions as divisive, discouraging and downright humiliating.

Roffey (2001: 6) emphasises the importance of the child being seen as a 'whole person'. She goes on to say:

> Where the child's difficulties and their remediation are the overwhelming focus for the entire family there is a danger that normal elements of functioning are ignored, possibly with negative consequences for the child's well-being in other areas. Collaboration and communication between parents, teachers and professionals will not only help to identify intervention, but also ensure that the child's needs are seen in the context of her overall development.

Practice example E2

Jake said his first word at 18 months and seemed to be doing well in all areas of development. At around three years, however, the setting noticed he was only using a small number of words and in discussion with his parents he was referred to his local speech and language service by his health visitor. Jake had an initial speech and language assessment which showed that while his comprehension was within normal limits, his ability to use expressive language was badly delayed. His frustration around his inability to express himself was beginning also to affect his behaviour, especially towards other children.

Shortly after his assessment, he was offered a block of group therapy sessions to which his mother and key worker were also invited. The sessions focused on early language skills and gave his mother and his key worker lots of ideas about how to extend these activities at home and at nursery as well as the information needed to set appropriate targets for him.

Makaton training was then delivered by the speech therapist to the whole setting and a Common Assessment Framework (CAF) meeting was set up so that professionals could liaise on the future needs of Jake and his family. As a result of these strategies Jake's vocabulary slowly improved and the use of Makaton signs reduced his frustration significantly so that he became much more sociable and was able to form relationships with other children.

Philippa Russell (in Carpenter and Egerton 2005) highlights the lack of longitudinal studies that assess the effectiveness of different models of early intervention and asks how we can ensure that there is more reliable evidence about the longer term effectiveness of particular programmes without this. In 2013 the national Early Intervention Foundation was founded which aims to create a standard of evidence for early intervention work and provide advice and guidance.

Entitlement

The notion of entitlement as opposed to a focus on 'need' can usefully underpin the development of inclusive practice. The idea that some children might have special, additional or different needs is often used to imply a deficiency on the part of those individual children and promote a view of them as passive rather than active recipients. In contrast, the concept of entitlement for all children ensures that no group of children is set apart from the population of children as a whole. Essentially, all children are seen as having the same entitlements and these are non-negotiable, whatever the context or situation. It is up to all the adults involved with the child to recognise these entitlements and ensure that they are met appropriately.

The term is used in relation to the United Nations Convention on the Rights of the Child (UNCRC), which underpins the moves that many countries are making towards inclusive practice including the UK. Within this framework it is recognised that, although needs may vary across cultures and settings, rights are a universal concept. All children, for example, should be entitled to education, be well fed, physically active, mentally stimulated and safe from physical and emotional harm.

In 1998 members of the Early Childhood Forum (ECF), an umbrella group facilitated by the National Children's Bureau, used the notion of entitlement as part of their *Quality in Diversity in Early Learning* framework (ECF 1998). They set out a number of entitlements that they think should provide a sound basis for children's early learning and development. These include familiar, consistent and sympathetic practitioners who work with families in an atmosphere of trust and respect and have high expectation of all children's developing capabilities.

References

Allen, G. (2011) *Early Intervention: The Next steps*. London: HMSO.

C4EO (2010) *Grasping the Nettle: Early Intervention for Children, Families and Communities*. London: National Children's Bureau.

Carpenter, B. and Egerton, J. (2005) *Early Childhood Intervention – International Perspectives*. Coventry: West Midlands SEN Regional Partnership.

Department for Education and Skills (DfES, 2003a) *Together From the Start: Practical Guidance for Professionals Working with Disabled Children (Birth to Third Birthday) and their Families*. London: DfES.

Department for Education and Skills (DfES, 2003b) *Every Child Matters*. London: HMSO.

Dickins, M. (2013) Supporting the well-being of disabled children and their families, in J. Manning-Morton (ed.) *Exploring Well-Being in the Early Years*. Maidenhead: Open University Press.

Dickins, M. with Denziloe, J. (2003) *All Together: How to Provide Inclusive Services for Disabled Children and their Families*. London: National Children's Bureau.

Early Childhood Forum (ECF, 1998) *Quality in Diversity in Early Learning – A Framework for Early Childhood Practitioners*. London: National Children's Bureau.

Early Intervention Foundation (2013) www.earlyinterventionfoundation.org.uk/ (accessed 19 May 2013).

Goddard Blythe, S. (2008) *What Babies and Children Really Need*. Stroud: Hawthorn Press.

Roffey, S. (2001) *Special Needs in the Early Years*. London: David Fulton.

Seigal, D.J. (1999) *The Developing Mind: Towards a Neurobiology of Interpersonal Experience*. New York: Guilford Press.

Sylva, K., Melhuish, E., Sammons, P., Siraj Blatchford, I. and Taggart, B. (2004) *The Effective Provision of Pre-School Education Project (EPPE): Final Report – A Longitudinal Study*. Nottingham: DfES Publications.

Wolfendale, S. (2000) *Special Educational Needs in the Early Years: Snapshots of Practice*. London: Routledge Falmer.

F

Families
Food

Families

There are many ideas about what constitutes a successful family which are constantly shifting and changing according to changes in society and how we choose to live our lives. In most societies the idea of the stereotypical heterosexual nuclear family still prevails and is supported by the media, education and religion. Historically, it is a traditional view of the family that has underpinned much of social policy. Prevailing ideas about how families are best constituted, arranged and maintained have not come about by accident. Banton et al. (2000: 90) note:

> Such a romantic and idealised view of the family is one which is often perceived as the norm in British life, perpetuated by pervasive media images and political ideologies. From such a perspective, the isolated nuclear family is well-suited to the needs of a modern industrial society. It is typically isolated, not being directly part of a wider kinship and therefore mobile and adaptable, thus suiting the needs of the labour market and the specialist functional units of society which have arisen as a result of industrialisation.

From a sociological and in particular a 'functionalist' perspective, which sees society as a whole system of functioning parts, the family is often viewed as a potential agency for social cohesion and stability. This view is reflected in policy. The American sociologist Talcott Parsons (cited in Banton et al. 2000: 89) describes the family as having 'basic and irreducible functions' which include:

- The rearing and socialising of children in order that they in turn will become productive adults and contribute to the smooth running of society.

- To provide physical and emotional support to the male workforce, thereby ensuring that the material needs of society are met.
- The stabilising of adult personalities of the population in order to prevent threat and disruption to the integrity of society as a whole.

Although, over the years, these ideas about the family have been substantially challenged, stereotypical ideas about what constitutes a successful family are still common (Albon 2007). Research (Smallwood and Wilson 2007) found that families headed by a married couple fell by half a million between 1996 and 2006, to just over 12 million. At the same time both lone-mother and cohabiting couple families increased so that they now total 2.3 million each. However, a study (Jenkins et al. 2009) found that there is still strong public support for the ideal of marriage across all social classes, especially where children are concerned. Lumsden and Doyle (2005: 168) make the point that: 'Children's experience of family life in the twenty-first century is one of diversity. There have been many changes to family structure, views about marriage have altered and the composition of society reflects differences of culture, ethnicity and religion.'

In modern societies it is clear that many families and individuals find themselves living in ways that do not correspond to traditional stereotypes. These may include reconstituted families in which death, divorce or the breakdown of a partnership have meant new relationships; same sex relationships; those in the care system without families or with substitute families; or anyone who has chosen to live outside a traditional framework or family system.

Defining what constitutes a family has therefore become more complex. Davidoff et al. (1999) have attempted to indicate the different ways in which family groups have historically related to each other and have identified the following strands or commonalities adapted below:

- **Kinship:** a group of blood relatives which extends over the generations, and amongst whom individuals have obligations and duties, even if they do not get on with each other.
- **Household:** a group of people who actually live together and share their lives. They are adults who are important in the lives of children in the household and may include nannies, lodgers, friends, guests, as well as relatives. The household could also represent adults of second marriages and the children of some or both of them.
- **Contractual relationships:** the marriage contract is a legal relationship which brings obligations with it. The legal structure of the upbringing of children is based on this relationship.
- **Loving relationship:** In the west today a marriage relationship often stems from romantic love. The family is seen as a place of nurture and loving relationship between parents and children.

Importantly, we should note that parents are not necessarily biologically linked to their children. The parenting role can be assumed by caring friends, step-parents, foster or adoptive parents or in some cases the state itself. Children may also have been conceived using IVF or other methods of assisted conception, such as donor insemination. The prevailing view that children are most likely to thrive in an intact, biological married home is called into question by current research which suggests that children of same-sex parents, for example, fare comparably (Goldberg 2009; Gartrell and Bos 2010).

Dallos and Sapsford (1997: 156) describe the considerable variations within UK culture in what might constitute family life. They see the nature of the modern day families as determined by a complex web of factors and make the point that the nuclear family is 'structured around financial dependence'. This raises the issue of how much the nature of the family unit and the way we live as families is determined by factors outside our control. They believe that much of social policy and the provision of social benefits still assumes that a woman is dependent on a male. Dallos and Sapsford (1997: 164) go on to explore how the institution of the family helps us to achieve our own identity through:

- emotional support
- a sense of solidarity
- enabling us to locate ourselves within the social order
- enabling us to establish a social identity, e.g. class, ethnic grouping.

Whatever our personal belief systems and values and however we think the ideal family is constituted, the importance of working *respectfully* with families as fundamental to the successful education and care of young children should not be underestimated. As Lumsden and Doyle (2005: 168) point out:

> Despite the clear indications that in order to develop satisfactorily, children need an identifiable, reliable family in the early years, the form it takes can vary.... It is through the experience of a 'stable' family life that the family members are able to grow, flourish and meet their full potential.

All early years settings generally aim to be supportive of family life. However, support can take many forms and sometimes also be experienced as negative and unhelpful. For example, the emotional support that individual families might need in times of stress will vary enormously and can be experienced negatively, particularly if seen as intrusive or underpinned by assumptions that the family cannot cope. Dickins with Denziloe 2003: 95 use the example of parents of disabled children to illustrate some of the difficulties that arise:

> Parents of disabled children are sometimes alienated by the amount and quality of professional intervention they have already received. They are often seen as over-protective and anxious for their children and we must take account of situations and experiences in the past which may have given rise to these worries and insecurities, even if we are sometimes justified in considering their reactions to be inappropriate.

Practice example F1

Cross Keys Nursery has a system of home visiting in the nursery and also a key-person system which means that one of the practitioners in the setting is assigned to a particular family. The key person has the responsibility of developing a close relationship with the child and the family and attending all home visits with another practitioner. They take toys from the nursery for the child to play with and find out information such as favourite television programmes, food, toys and music.

The manager at Cross Keys overheard practitioners making negative comments about a child's home when they came back from a visit. In talking to parents about the home visiting experience she found out that some of them thought that the visit was also a hygiene inspection of their home and one parent had even decorated her front room because she knew the nursery staff were visiting. The manager held a parents meeting and developed a leaflet which made clear the role of the home visit, stressing that it was not an inspection. She also held an inset training day for practitioners so that they were clear about the need for respectful engagement with families and the remit of the home visit.

There is no doubt that difficulties can be overcome. Sensitivity, power sharing and the awareness and maturity to be able to learn directly from individual families can enhance and positively develop working practice with families and improve outcomes for all children.

Food

Across all cultures and traditions sharing food together is a sign of acceptance and a stepping stone to building positive relationships. Lane (2008) points out that mealtimes and eating are also an opportunity to learn about other culinary traditions and the culture and practices of the people who eat them. However, what we eat and how we eat it can be a potential minefield for the child and family who are perceived of as different. The whole issue of which implements to use and how food is consumed is culturally and socially loaded. In considering food, identity and ethnicity, Albon and Mukherji (2010: 101-2) point out:

> What is defined as a food is, itself, a social construction...By this we mean that what is considered edible or not, and the meanings ascribed to certain foods, are situated within a particular culture and within a certain point in time...maintaining a sense of one's cultural identity through food is important, especially to people who have migrated to a new country.

Photograph F1   Mealtimes as a social occasion

Although healthy eating is desirable and to be encouraged, there is nothing inherently superior in any particular food or in the way people choose to eat it. However, being treated as though the food that you like is somehow different or unpleasant and/or the way you eat it is somehow wrong can be damaging to your sense of self and your pride in your culture especially when you are very young.

McAuliffe and Lane (2011: 4) stress that as the food that children eat and like will reflect their family and cultural backgrounds, acknowledging the food eaten by each child can help them feel as though they belong. They point out that in order to teach children to respect and value diversity we need to do the following:

- recognise and understand how and why children may be prejudiced against, and make stereotypical assumptions about, people who are different from themselves and, consequently, may see the food they eat as inferior to their own;
- give positive messages about differences in order to undermine these assumptions, as well as providing opportunities for them to unlearn any negative attitudes that they may have learnt.

Albon and Mukherji (2010: 126) point out that practitioners also need to think about gender in relation to food and eating. They cite a study (Ludvigsen and Sharma 2004), intriguingly titled *Burger Boy and Sporty Girl,* in which primary school children were shown a picture of a burger, chips and coke and another picture of a

Photograph F2 A chance to try something new

more healthy meal option. Children were asked to describe in detail the person they thought might eat these meals. A strong gender divide became evident and they noted that the children thought that 'only very wealthy, clever, sporty girls' could ever be imagined as choosing a healthy lunch and that 'real' boys definitely do not eat healthy food (Ludvigsen and Sharma 2004: 25).

Eating together can be especially challenging for some disabled children. They may experience physical difficulties such as motor impairment, lack of control or inability to swallow. Emotional and behavioural difficulties sometimes include food refusal or throwing food and there may be specific conditions such as allergies or, as in Prader-Willi syndrome, a constant desire to eat. Challenges for the adults involved may include the following:

- Responding positively to impairment and physical difference (attitude).
- Responding positively to perceived 'bad' table manners and behaviour.

- Responding positively to 'messiness'.
- Allowing disabled children to take the time they need.
- Communication and listening, especially when tending to likes and dislikes.
- Enabling the peer group of children and parents to respond positively to these differences.

Practice example F2

Jennifer is three and a half and currently has a naso-gastric tube for feeding although the eventual aim is for her to be able to have food orally. The mother explains that at home they all still sit and eat together and even take turns to have an empty plate in front of them so that Jennifer does not feel excluded. The staff work with Jennifer on oral feeding even through this is time consuming and difficult.

The parent has this to say about their efforts: 'The goal was to have the tube out. It hasn't worked but they've done a lot of work on oral feeding. I remember one day a nursery nurse came home with her and told me she'd eaten all her dinner. I couldn't believe it, so the nursery nurse came back in her own time and helped me feed Jennifer.'

The support she receives from the setting has meant that Jennifer's mother feels able to persevere with the oral feeds, even though they are frustrating and hard work.

All too often disabled children who eat differently are given their meals separately and yet the value of social eating is universally recognised and valued. It is important that disabled children are not denied the opportunity to interact socially, to make choices, to learn how to use utensils, to acquire knowledge about social rules and conventions and most of all to feel that they belong and are able to participate as fully as possible in all aspects of the life of the setting.

References

Albon, D. (2007) Working with parents and careres, in J. Moyles (ed) *Beginning Teaching, Beginning Learning*. Maidenhead: Open University Press.

Albon, D. and Mukherji, P. (2010) *Food and Health in Early Childhood*. London: Sage.

Banton, R., Fenwick, G. and Hawtin, A. (2000) The family, in D. Wyse and A. Hawton (eds) *Children: A Multidisciplinary Perspective*. London: Arnold.

Dallos, R. and Sapsford, R. (1997) Patterns of diversity and lived realities, in J. Muncie, M. Weatherall, M. Langan, R. Dallos and A.D. Cochrane (eds) (1997) *Understanding the Family*. London: Sage.

Davidoff, L., Doolittle, M., Fink, J. and Holden, K. (1999) *The Family Story.* London: Longman.

Dickins, M. with Denziloe, J. (2003) *All Together: How to Provide Inclusive Services for Disabled Children and their Families.* London: National Children's Bureau.

Gartrell, N. and Bos, H. (2010) US national longitudinal lesbian family study: psychological adjustment of 17-year-old adolescents, *Pediatrics,* 126: 28–36.

Goldberg, A. (2009) *Lesbian and Gay Parents and their Children: Research on the Family Life Cycle.* Washington, DC: APA Books.

Jenkins, S., Periera, I. and Evan, N. (2009) *Families in Britain: The Impact of Changing Family Structures and What the Public think.* London: Ipsos Mori/ Policy Exchange.

Lane, J. (2008) *Young Children and Racial Justice.* London: National Children's Bureau.

Ludvigsen, A. and Sharma, N. (2004) *Burger Boy and Sporty Girl: Children and Young People's Attitude Towards Food in School.* Ilford: Barnardo's.

Lumsden, E. and Doyle, C. (2005) Working with families, in Waller (ed.) *An Introduction to Early Childhood.* London: Sage.

McAuliffe, A. and Lane, J. (2011) *Listening and Responding to Young Children's Views on Food.* London: National Children's Bureau.

Smallwood, S. and Wilson, B. (2007) *Focus on Families.* London: Office for National Statistics.

G

Gender equality

Gender equality (sometimes described as gender equity) in the early years is all about developing proactive principles, policy and practice that positively advantage, rather than disadvantage, babies and young children in their development and learning on the basis of their gender. The broader vision is for an education system that ensures that all children, male and female can be engaged and effective learners across a broad curriculum, have high expectations of themselves and others, and be prepared for fulfilling lives that have not been hindered by gender stereotyping and fixed expectations on the basis of whether they are a boy or a girl. In short, children should be able to fulfil themselves as individuals, positively embracing all the diverse aspects of themselves that make up their unique identity.

It is important to recognise the meanings of the terms 'sex' and 'gender' because the two are often confused. Sex is the biological term used to describe the biological differences between males and female. Genetic sex differences between males and females lead to hormonal differences and therefore differences in size and shape and reproductive organs. Although it is usually assumed that all boys have XY chromosomes and all girls have XX and that sex can be identified easily, a small minority of children are born with XO chromosomes and/or have ambiguous genitalia.

Gender is the term that describes all the different aspects of being male or female which are not attributable to biological differences. It takes in psychological and cultural expectations and differences in behaviour, abilities, qualities and attitudes between men and women. The expression of the differences between men and women will vary from culture to culture. Differences in gender might be indicated by different styles and items of clothing, different hairstyles, different temperaments and personality characteristics and different expectations about career and occupation. The term 'gender identity' is used to describe an internalisation of the roles and behaviours associated with being feminine or masculine; not all females are 'feminine' and not all males are 'masculine' so these differences are not dependent on sex.

Gender stereotyping occurs when we have fixed ideas and beliefs about what it means to be male or female. Gender stereotypes about children are based on information about aspects such as appearance, interests, attitudes, dispositions and social and psychological traits. To some degree all of us will have internalised ideas about what it means to be male or female and what constitutes gender stereotypical behaviour for boys and girls. Golombok and Fivush (1994: 18) explain further:

> When we consider the combination of traits describing males and females, these clusters of traits can be conceptualized as describing two distinct orientations towards the world. Males are stereotypically considered to be agentive or instrumental; they act on the world and make things happen. Females are stereotypically relational; they are concerned with social interaction and emotions.

Golombok and Fivush see gender stereotypes as representing a set of culturally shared beliefs and suggests that value judgements are constantly being made as a result about what are considered socially desirable and appropriate behaviours.

Practice example G1

Liam is four. He attends a playgroup in a small village and has three older sisters. When he started attending the setting at the age of three he showed little interest in block play, climbing or super-hero games that the other boys regularly enjoyed. He preferred instead to look at books, to engage in small world play and to play at dressing up in the home corner. His mother commented on this and staff tried to actively encourage him to play more with the other boys. Liam resisted this pressure and made it clear that he did not enjoy boisterous 'rough and tumble' play. Engaging with Liam and observing that he is a happy child who is developing well and socialises well with both boys and girls raises awareness in the staff about the gender divide of activities and this is adjusted so that girls and boys are encouraged to access the full range of activities.

In considering the forces and influences that determine both our individuality and our 'sameness', much of the discussion about gender issues still centres on the nature versus nurture debate concerning to what extent and how the environment we are born into, including belief systems, values and social and cultural frameworks, determines who we eventually become. Despite advances in neuroscience and an enormous body of research, the only scientific consensus is that we cannot project from babyhood anything certain about the development of children's minds based on their gender. What follows here is a brief outline and exploration of the main theories that cannot possibly do justice to the wealth of writing and research in this complex area.

Social learning theory and theorists such as Bandura (1977) maintain that children are shaped into developing what is considered to be sex-appropriate behaviour through the observation of the behaviour of adults, especially parents, but will also imitate the behaviour of people of the same sex, for example, boys imitating the aggressive behaviour of male figures on the television. This explanation has been criticised as ignoring the many different messages that children receive from different sources, some of which are actively resisted. MacNaughton (2000: 21) calls this the 'sponge model' of identity formation and says that it fails to address the following questions:

- How do children construct their social understandings from the competing understandings of gender, race, class, etc. with which various social institutions present them?
- To what extent do they construct their ideas in the ways intended by such institutions?

Researchers have observed that young children can hold very rigid views on what is gender appropriate or not. One explanation for this is cognitive developmental theory of whom Kohlberg (1966) is the best known proponent. Kohlberg believed that the child's level of cognitive development is the most important factor in children's development of gender identity. As the child is labelled a boy or girl, they begin to view themselves as masculine or feminine. Alongside this sense of gender identity is the child's growing knowledge and understanding of gender which affects their way of thinking and behaving, that is, 'I am a girl – I must behave like a girl.'

Browne (2004: 72) sees this theory as failing to explain why older children and adolescents may also hold rigid views: 'The theory [therefore] fails to take adequate account of the range of styles of femininity and masculinities a child may adopt and the power of different discourses in determining in the child's mind, what is "gender appropriate" and what is "gender inappropriate".'

There have been many studies examining social influences on gender development. People seem to view even newborn babies differently according to their sex. In a study conducted by Rubin et al. (1974) parents were asked to describe their newborn babies as if they were talking to a friend. The study found that boys were more likely to be described as strong, alert and well coordinated. Conversely, the girls tended to be described as smaller and softer even though the babies were similar in health, weight and size.

Nurseries and schools have been found to reinforce and encourage sex stereotyped behaviour and attitudes in young children, albeit unintentionally at times. Dweck and her co-researchers (1978) looked at the different experiences of boys and girls in the classroom. They examined the type of feedback received by boys and girls in a maths lesson and found that boys tended to get more negative feedback than girls. The 'hidden message' behind the feedback was that the problems which the boys were experiencing with their work were due to factors such as not listening carefully rather than intellectual incompetence. Although girls in the study received less negative feedback, the positive feedback they received rarely focused on their mathematical achievements. The study concluded that boys were more likely to perceive themselves to be mathematicians.

Birch and Malim (1988) summed up the many studies looking at the development of gender and concluded that there was no single process responsible for gender-role development. They felt that biological factors, for example, sex hormones, play some part in predisposing children to behaviours viewed as masculine and feminine and that the child's own perception of their gender and the reinforcement from other people of what is considered to be sex-appropriate behaviour are important factors. Sex stereotyping on the television and in books, etc., as well as among peers and in the family is also likely to be a factor in gender development. In summary, the differences between children in terms of their gender development may arise from both genetic predispositions and the influence of people, culture and situations. In other words nature and nurture both play an important part.

Writers who take a feminist perspective in their analyses of children's gender development such as MacNaughton (2000: 234) and Holland (2003) question commonly held 'truths' about gender, such as the following:

- Gender is fixed and immutable.
- Good early childhood practice inherently produces equitable outcomes for all children.
- Gender is not an issue in early childhood settings.
- Young children don't know or don't care about gender.

Whatever our personal and professional views about gender development, practitioners need to recognise that girls frequently miss out on the experiences offered by construction activities and mechanical and wheeled toys. This type of play helps to develop the skills and concepts necessary for mathematics, science and technology. Many early years workers are women who themselves may have little experience of playing with these toys. Girls may well notice this and be discouraged from having a go. Female early years educators need to develop confidence with these activities to be able to support girls in their endeavours.

The root of boys' underachievement has been traced back to the early years by some commentators who see signs of boys' lack of interest in early and pre-literacy activities as a significant contribution to their underachievement in later years. In *Boys and Girls: Superheroes in the Doll Corner*, Vivian Gussin Paley (1984) observed that her classroom was a female-dominated space with its focus on table-top literacy based activities which appear to exclude boys. She describes how she supported boys' use of narrative by creating the space for them to talk about their fantasy world of superheroes. This strategy draws boys in on their own terms to the world of early literacy.

The feminist perspective is important here for several reasons. A feminist view emphasises women's role as carers in both the formal professional sphere as well as the informal unpaid sphere (Dale and Foster 1986). The feminist critique also highlights the low status and pay of childcare and childcare workers owing to the perceived view that childcare is women's work and that women need only to deploy the 'talents' they use in the home to be a childcare professional (Mahon 2002). Also highlighted by the feminist perspective is how everyday teaching practices such as the early childhood curriculum and pedagogy all influence the development of young children's gender identities (MacNaughton 2000).

Holland (2003) asserts how the predominance of early years pedagogy aimed at lessening the growth in male aggression, in particular the enforcement of zero-tolerance policies towards superhero war and weapon play, has served to alienate young boys as 'other' in early childhood settings. In other words, noisy, lively, physical play is not accorded the same value as the compliant, quiet and passive play sometimes associated with girls.

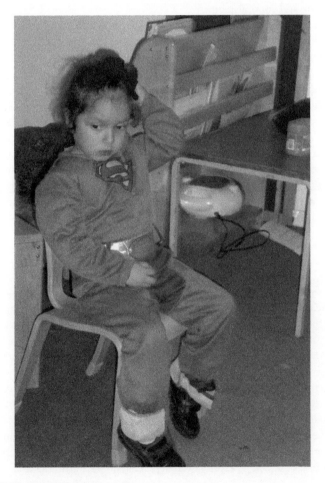

Photograph G1   Superman takes a break

The way that adults respond to children's choices of activity must be acknowledged; for example, practitioners should be careful not to only reward children for gender-appropriate behaviours. The primary focus must be the provision of an enabling environment for each child; getting to know individual children without bias or expectation; and the use of activities and resources that positively reflect the diversity and possibilities that exist in society.

Groundwork

In order for a setting to become inclusive it is crucial that the groundwork has been done so that all members of the team have the necessary underpinning knowledge, understanding and commitment.

One way to start is with a practice audit which will allow you to gather information about how inclusive your setting or service is at the moment. The audit should be designed to answer key questions as to whether your setting is currently representative of the community; allows equal access to the environment; curriculum; physical activities; outings and events; and whether there are issues regarding race and gender equality which need to be addressed. It should identify the existing strengths and weaknesses of the service and signpost any special equipment, staff and adaptations that will be needed to support any additional needs the children may have. You will also need to scrutinise existing policies, practice and procedures to ensure that they are not contradictory or exclusive and have taken into account up-to-date guidance and legislation. Exploring issues that staff members may find difficult to talk about will not be easy, but if we are to tackle inequality and injustice in our settings, and indeed in wider society, it is crucial that we do so.

Practice example G2

After being criticised by Ofsted for a lack of inclusivity in their approach, Bright Start nursery undertook a comprehensive practice audit. They found that existing staff and parents had never had ready access to their policy on inclusion or contributed to it. Although staff were willing and eager to include children with a range of difficulties, they lacked knowledge and confidence, particularly around conditions such as epilepsy and autistic spectrum disorder.

The current special educational needs coordinator (SENCo) then voiced her unhappiness – feeling that children with additional needs were left entirely up to her and that other staff should also take responsibility for them. With the support of the area SENCo she developed and implemented a training programme designed to create awareness, change staff attitudes and develop skills and confidence. The manager and staff did their best to access multi-agency support from health and social services and to link with voluntary sector organisations that could also offer support and advice. With these measures in place, staff, parents and children were involved in putting together an attractive and accessible policy document which they reviewed on a regular basis.

As a result of this process, over many weeks, staff had a much better understanding of their own strengths and weaknesses and the need to identify needs systematically at an early stage and to design effective interventions and monitor children's progress. In time they became a 'hub' of expertise and were able to offer training and support to other settings in their area.

A good policy is a working document and a statement of the vision, beliefs, values and goals of a setting. It should ensure consistency in practice and give a common message to practitioners, parents, children and anyone else who comes into contact with the setting or service. Self-scrutiny will always be a necessary part of this process. For example, questions about disability that teams could initially consider include the following (Dickins with Denziloe 2003: 51):

- What is disability?
- Is society afraid of disability? Why?
- Are we afraid of disability? Why?
- What are our training and support needs and how can they be met?
- What support do disabled children need and how can we provide it?
- What support is needed by parents of non-disabled children to help them understand our policies?

It is always important to hold in mind that inclusion is a process through which we are continually learning about how best to impart a sense of belonging and participation to the children in our care. Each new child and family that walks through the door is likely to bring with them new and perhaps unforeseen, complexities and challenges.

References

Bandura, A. (1977) *Social Learning Theory.* Upper Saddle River, NJ: Prentice Hall.
Birch, A. and Malim, T. (1988) *Developmental Psychology From Infancy to Adulthood.* Bristol: Intertext Limited.
Browne, N. (2004) *Gender Equity in the Early Years.* Maidenhead: Open University Press.
Dale, J. and Foster, P. (1986) *Feminists and State Welfare.* London: Routledge and Kegan Paul.
Dickins, M. with Denziloe, J. (2003) *All Together: How to Create Inclusive Services for Disabled Children and their Families.* London: National Children's Bureau.

Dweck, C.S., Davidson, W., Nelson, S. and Enna, B. (1978) Sex differences in learned help-lessness: (II) The contingencies of evaluative feedback in the classroom and (III) An experimental analysis, *Developmental Psychology*, 14: 268–276.

Golombok, S. and Fivush, R. (1994) *Gender Development.* Cambridge: Cambridge University Press.

Gussin Paley, V. (1984) *Boys and Girls: Superheroes in the Doll Corner.* Chicago: University of Chicago Press.

Holland, P. (2003) *We Don't Play with Guns Here: War, Weapon and Super Hero Play in the Early Years.* Maidenhead: Open University Press.

Kohlberg, L. (1966) A cognitive developmental analysis of children's sex role concepts and attitudes, in E. Maccoby *The Development of Sex Differences.* Stanford, CT: Stanford University Press.

MacNaughton, G. (2000) *Rethinking Gender in Early Childhood Education.* London: Paul Chapman.

Mahon, R. (2002) Introduction, in S. Michel and R. Mahon (eds) *Child Care Policy at the Crossroads: Gender and Welfare State Restructuring.* London: Routledge

Rubin, J.S., Provenzano, F. J. and Luria, Z. (1974) The eye of the beholder: parents' view on sex of newborns, *American Journal Of Orthopsychiatry*, 5: 353–363.

H

Health
Health inequality
HIV
Housing

Health

The World Health Organization (1946) defines health as: 'a state of complete physical, mental and social wellbeing and not merely the absence of infirmity'. Although this definition implies a holistic perception of health, it has been widely criticised as being too idealistic, unattainable and undifferentiated, in that it implies that all positive aspects of life are elements of good health. It also fails to take account of the myriad differences between human beings as individuals. Nevertheless, it does incorporate a positive model of health as opposed to a negative one in which health is merely the absence of disease.

Another related model that is prevalent in relation to discussions about health is the biomedical model which has been dominant for most of this century. From a biomedical perspective, particular emphasis is placed on the biological causes and manifestations of disease and ill health. The social model of health, by contrast, sees the health of individuals and communities as the result of complex interacting forces such as social and economic status and environmental and personal factors. A definition of health that is often used to support this view is that of Seedhouse (1988) for whom a person's optimum state of health is equivalent to the state of the set of conditions which fulfil or enable that person to work to fulfil his or her chosen and biological potential. According to Karstadt and Medd (2000: 73), Seedhouse sees health as:

> ...existing on a continuum, with different degrees of health being reached at a given point in time. He describes a set of central conditions and suggests that the degree to which these are met will provide

a foundation for the achievement of our potential. These conditions include food, drink, shelter, warmth, purpose in life, access to information about factors which affect life, the ability to use this information, and an understanding that we live and exist within the context of our environment and community.

The social model sees health primarily as the responsibility of society as a whole. From this perspective we all have a collective and individual responsibility with regard to public and personal health. This view is important when we begin to explore health inequalities because it leads to a focus on the functions and responsibilities of societies to provide the right conditions for health.

For any young child that requires a high degree of physical care, sensitivity, respect and responsiveness from carers will be essential to their overall well-being. The building of trust through positive physical interactions is a fundamental aspect of developing healthy close relationships with other people and if staff are uncomfortable with the processes this can give a damaging message to the child. Greenman and Stonehouse (1996: 108) suggest the following general guidelines when caring for the physical needs of any child:

- Keeping the importance of children developing a positive self-concept uppermost in your mind.
- Avoiding talking to other staff about the children as if they were not there.
- Do not let your own attitudes to food, bodily waste or dirt make a caring time negative for a child. Avoid using words like dirty or smelly.
- Paying attention to your body language, voice tone and the way you handle children and remember the messages that each of these will convey to the child and how they will make the child feel.

Practitioners will sometimes hear the terms 'complex needs' or 'complex health needs' used in relation to individual children. There is not yet an agreed definition of 'complex needs' but this category would normally include babies and children who have needs in one or more developmental area (e.g. motor, sensory, communication, learning, social skills) and who might also have continuing health needs, home nursing needs, be dependent on technological support, or have uncertain or short life expectancy.

Examples of the care or health needs of children in this category might include a child with a tracheostomy who requires regular airway suctioning during the day, a child who requires a gastronomy or tube feed at mealtimes, or a child who requires assistance with bladder emptying and needs catheterisation at each break time.

Practice example H1

Divine is extremely nervous when she becomes the key worker for Darren, who is four, because he has been diagnosed with severe epilepsy and has experienced two prolonged seizures in the past at home. Darren's mother explains that his condition is largely under control with medication and explains the signs, such as disorientation, that Darren experiences prior to a seizure. Once Divine has learnt exactly what to do if a seizure occurs, she feels much more confident about the situation.

Children with complex health needs have the same rights of admission to school or setting as other children and cannot generally be excluded from school for health reasons. Some children with a high level of complex and/or severe needs may begin their schooling in special provision and others may find themselves in an assessment nursery where there may be a higher level of staff expertise. Including children with complex health needs in ordinary settings may require time to plan and make reasonable adjustments or to put into place appropriate support arrangements.

Each school and early years setting should have in place a policy and protocols on supporting children with complex health needs. Carlin (2005) emphasises the importance of fulfilling the anticipatory duties required by equality law. This means that settings should be thinking ahead about what adjustments and measures might be needed to support individual children who might want to attend. The process of designing and implementing a policy will help to identify any training and specialist support and advice needs, fears and anxieties and demonstrate commitment to positively promoting inclusive practice. It will also lead to a clear understanding of the roles and responsibilities of staff within a school or early years setting; clarify for parents and children what they can expect from the school or early years settings and what is expected from them. Settings may require time to plan and make reasonable adjustments or to put into place support arrangements.

Practice example H2

Harry, who is three, has had attacks of asthma since he was a few months old. His childminder, Ruth, has been careful to get to know the environmental triggers he experiences such as cleaning materials, dog hair and the chlorine in swimming pools, and to take steps to avoid these and other factors which exacerbate his condition. Harry is encouraged to ask for his medication when he needs it and it is always kept readily accessible.

There will always be practitioners who are uncomfortable with the idea of performing certain physical and medical procedures and it is a sound role of thumb that no one should ever be forced to do so if they clearly do not want to. Whilst training and support can lead to new skills and knowledge, the worst scenario is to give a child the message that practitioners find any aspect of caring for them messy, scary or uncomfortable. For many practitioners, however, such skills and knowledge are a valuable and rewarding addition to their repertoire.

Health inequality

In its literal sense the term 'health inequality' means the differences in health status between individuals or groups as measured by factors such as life expectancy, mortality, disease or impairment. Enormous inequalities exist globally in terms of children's health, despite advances in technology and increasing knowledge about disease transmission. The links between economic and social status and health inequalities in the UK are well established. The Marmot Review (Marmot 2011: 10) states:

> Inequalities in health arise because of inequalities in society – in the conditions in which people are born, grow, live, work and age. So close is the link between particular social and economic features of society and the distribution of health across the population, that the magnitude of health inequalities is a good marker of progress towards creating a fairer society. Taking action to reduce inequalities in health does not require a separate health agenda, but action across the whole of society.

Being poor and unequal is recognised as having negative consequences for all aspects of physical and mental health and as having profound effects on the health of children. There is a large body of research that indicates that the poorer the child the more likely they are to have health problems and increased rates of disability and ill health. It is also clear that the health of the mother has a profound effect on the health of her children. (Acheson 1998; Meltzer et al. 2000). Furthermore there are indications that health inequality in the UK is increasing alongside other aspects of inequality. Research by the London Health Observatory commissioned by the Marmot Review Team in 2012 built on the original Marmot Review and showed that health inequalities are widening within most areas of England (Child and Maternal Health Intelligence Network 2012).

The right of a child to health and health care is explored by Underdown (2007) who notes that this is alluded to directly and indirectly in many of the articles of the United Nations Convention on the Rights of the Child, and stresses our legal responsibility to fulfil this entitlement. This has been recognised in policy and legislation (Franklin 2002) such as *Every Child Matters* (DfES 2003) and the subsequent Children Act 2004. The overall health and well-being of young children is likely to be inextricable from their family and the stresses and anxieties which the family as a whole is undergoing. There is a wide of range of factors that can all impact on family life and result in negative health consequences for any family members, such as poverty and living conditions, domestic or substance abuse, unemployment or marital/partner separation.

The mental health of children is also a matter for particular concern. The *Bright Futures* report from the Mental Health Foundation (Kay 1999: 6) defines children's mental health as the ability to do the following:

- Develop psychologically, emotionally, creatively, intellectually and spiritually.
- Initiate, develop and sustain mutually satisfying personal relationships.
- Use and enjoy solitude.
- Become aware of others and empathise with them.
- Play and learn.
- Develop a sense of right and wrong.
- Face problems and setbacks and learn from them in ways appropriate for the child's age.

Kay (1999: 8) points out:

> There is no simple equation that will tell us where a particular child is going to face mental health problems . . . some children can live through the most traumatic experiences and maintain a sense of wellbeing while others who live in safe and caring environments will still face mental health problems.

Recent research has shown an increasing prevalence of mental health problems in children. According to the mental health charity Young Minds one in ten children and young people aged 5 to 16 suffer from a diagnosable mental health disorder (Young Minds 2013). These conditions include attachment disorders and separation anxiety; emotional disorders such as phobias and depression that are manifested in physical symptoms or anxiety; conduct disorders such as aggression and anti-social behaviours; hyperkinetic disorders such as attention or activity disorders; developmental disorders such as delayed speech and physical difficulties; post-traumatic stress syndrome and a range of other conditions which cause mental distress and inhibit social and emotional development.

There are many risk factors that can increase the probability of a child experiencing mental health problems. Risk factors that relate to the children themselves include specific learning and communication difficulties, developmental delay, genetic influences, physical illness, academic failure and low self-esteem. Factors in the family can include parental conflict and relationship breakdown, poor parenting skills, abusive relationships, substance addiction and abuse, and death and loss including loss of friendship. In addition to these factors there are also risk factors in the community including homelessness, trauma or disaster, experiencing discrimination and isolation and many other significant life events. Mental ill health and distress can be the result of a complex interplay between any or all of these factors.

Practice example H3

At Turnmill Nursery they have developed a fruit and vegetable garden where children can plant, nurture and harvest a wide variety of produce. The setting has an imaginative and varied snack menu that is clearly displayed to parents on the noticeboard. Children routinely help with the preparation of food.

The setting encourages parents to access activities such as community walks and there is a range of accessible indoor and outdoor physical activities available for the children. They have developed a movement chart that can be used to track individual children's outdoor and physical activity and have established clear and detailed monitoring of well-being and involvement levels. The setting nurtures positive relationships between children, parents and the local community through fund raising events and an annual open day where produce is sold.

There is much that early years practitioners can do to promote the health and well-being of children and families; for example, the provision of good-quality holistic care for children which not only takes account of physical needs such as food, drink, exercise, rest and sleep, but also aims to fulfil social, intellectual and cultural entitlements. Practitioners can help children to learn to be independent and care for themselves by establishing health routines that will stay with them for life, such as appropriate handwashing. They can give children the knowledge and information to make healthy lifestyle choices and the confidence and opportunity to make healthy decisions for themselves. They can engage with parents on projects such as healthy eating and also act as an advocate empowering them to access appropriate health provision for themselves and their families.

HIV

HIV, or the Human Immunodeficiency Virus, is a virus that attacks the immune system. AIDS (Acquired Immune Deficiency Syndrome) is an advanced stage of HIV infection, when a person's immune system is too weak to fight off a range of diseases with which it would normally cope. In the UK, HIV is most commonly transmitted through sex without a condom, between men and women, or men having sex with other men.

Some children are born with HIV which they acquire in utero, during birth or through breast milk. The virus can be passed on through infected blood, semen, vaginal fluids, rectal secretions or breast milk. It cannot be transmitted through any ordinary, everyday contact (NCB/HIV Network 2013).

Most children currently living with HIV in the UK have contracted it from their mothers at birth or through breastfeeding. The development of antiretroviral therapy in the past 15 to 20 years has dramatically improved the outcomes for children living with HIV in the UK. It is now suggested that HIV be regarded as a treatable chronic disease. Therefore, broadly speaking, most children living with HIV in the UK have a good health prognosis and most will survive their childhood and live well into adulthood.

In the past there has been great prejudice towards adults and children who are HIV positive. Such was the fear and lack of understanding that children with HIV were sometimes not admitted to early years settings. Now it is recognised that there is no danger that other children or staff will contract the disease if normal hygiene rules are followed. Children who are HIV positive may be more susceptible to infections, so it is important that parents and carers are informed if there is an infectious disease in the nursery.

Often parents do not want to share this information about their child with all and their right to privacy should be respected. The consequences of a breach of confidentiality can be extremely serious for families and can sometimes lead to social isolation and even harassment (DoH 1992).

Housing

Quality of housing can have a huge impact on well-being. Inadequate housing increases the risk of severe ill health and disability. It can also lead to poor mental health, lower educational attainment, unemployment and poverty. The importance of housing is recognised in the United Nations Covenant on Economic, Social and Cultural Rights, which includes 'the right of everyone to an adequate standard of living for himself and his family, including adequate housing'. The UK is legally bound by this treaty (EHRC 2011).

Despite this commitment, many young children are growing up in housing conditions that are insecure, overcrowded and of a poor standard. According to the campaigning housing charity Shelter UK (Harker 2006: 8) poor and inadequate housing brings with it the following risks for children:

- Up to 25 per cent higher risk of severe ill health and disability during childhood and early adulthood.
- Increased risk of meningitis, asthma, and slow growth, which is linked to coronary heart disease.
- A greater chance of suffering mental health problems and problems with behaviour.
- Lower educational attainment and greater likelihood of unemployment and poverty.

Underdown (2007: 66) draws attention to the fact that many UK families, especially those on low incomes, are living in overcrowded and substandard accommodation in areas of high pollution and often with poor quality amenities and services such as shops and transport. She points out that 'While the physical effects are perhaps the most obvious, there is also a wide range of more subtle and pervasive health issues linked with inadequate housing'.

There may, for example, be a lack of safe and accessible play areas (Gill 1992), or crime and drug use may have resulted in a threatening environment for children and families (Spencer 2000). There is growing evidence to show that current housing policy with means tested social housing tenancies and the cap on housing benefits are likely to cause significant displacement of families and widespread in-country migration (Lister et al. 2011).

Practice example H4

Marissa and her mother are staying in hostel accommodation having recently become homeless. Marissa's mother has become depressed about their situation, especially because she has to leave the accommodation in the daytime and finds it difficult to fill her time productively. Staff at Marissa's nursery explain that she is always welcome to spend time there, and suggest that she become a volunteer helper for three afternoons a week. This is a great success and the mother eventually enrols on a childcare course at a local college.

Studies on the effective provision of pre-school education (EPPE) such as Melhuish et al. (2001) stressed that although the socio-economic status of parents was important, the quality of the home learning environment (HLE) was even more important, and that what parents did was more important than who they were. However, it could be argued that if families do not have a stable and adequate home in the first place, the provision of a safe, appropriate and rich home environment will be infinitely more difficult to achieve.

References

Acheson, D. (1998) *Inequalities in Health: Report of an Independent Inquiry.* London: HMSO.

Carlin, J. (2005) *Including Me: Managing Complex Health Needs in Schools and Early Years Settings.* London: Council for Disabled Children.

Child and Maternal Health Unit (2012) *Marmot Indicators for Local Authorities in England.* www.iho.org.uk/LHO_Topics/national_lead_areas/marmot/marmotindicators.aspx (accessed 12 July 2013).

Department for Education and Skill (DfES, 2003) *Every Child Matters.* London: HMSO.

Department of Health (DoH 1992) *Children and HIV: Guidance for Local Authorities.* London: HMSO.

Equality and Human Rights Commission (EHRC, 2011) *Human Rights at Home: Guidance for Social Housing Providers.* www.equalityhumanrights.com/human-rights/human-rights -practical-guidance/guidance-from-the-commission/human-rights-at-home/ (accessed 11 April 2013).

Franklin, B. (ed.) (2002) *The New Handbook of Children's Rights*. London: Routledge Meltzer.

Gill, T. (1992) *Parenting under Pressure*. London: Barnardos.

Greenman, J. and Stonehouse, A. (1996) *Prime Times: A Handbook for Excellence in Infant and Toddler Programs*. St. Paul, MN: Redleaf Press.

Harker, L. (2006) *Chance of a Lifetime: The Impact of Bad Housing on Children's Lives*. London: Shelter.

Karstadt, L. and Medd, J. (2000) Promoting child health, in R., Drury, L. Miller and S. Kirk (eds) *Looking at Early Years Education and Care*. London: David Fulton.

Kay, H. (1999) *Bright Futures - Promoting Children and Young People's Mental Health*. London: Mental Health Foundation.

Lister, S., Reynolds, L. and Webb, K. (2011) *The Impact of the Welfare Reform Bill on Affordability for Low Income Private Renting Families*. London: Shelter.

Marmot, M. (2011) *Fair Society, Healthy Lives: The Marmot Review*. London: London Health Observatory.

Melhuish, E., Sylva, C., Sammons, P., Siraj-Blatchford, I. and Taggart, B. (2001) *Social, Behavioural and Cognitive Development at 3–4 Years in relation to Family Background. The Effective Provision of Pre-school Education, EPPE Project*. London: Institute of Education.

Meltzer, H., Gatword, R., with Goodman, R. and Ford, T. (2000) *The Mental Health of Children and Adolescents in Great Britain*. London: Office for National Statistics.

National Children's Bureau/HIV Network. www.ncb.org.uk/studying-with-hiv/introducing-hiv (accessed 3 May 2013).

Seedhouse, D. (1988) *Ethics: The Heart of Health Care*. Chichester: Wiley.

Spencer, N. (2000) *Poverty and Child Health*, 2nd ed. Oxford: Radcliffe Medical Press.

Underdown, A. (2007) *Young Children's Health and Well-being*. Maidenhead: Open University Press.

World Health Organization (WHO, 1946) *Preamble to the Constitution of the World Health Organization* as adopted by the International Health Conference, New York, 19–22 June 1946; entered into force 7 April 1948. Geneva: WHO.

Young Minds (2013) *Statistics on Mental Health*. www.youngminds.org.uk/training_services/policy/mental_health_statistics (accessed 19 May 2013).

I

Inequality

There are many kinds of inequality, but this section is focused largely on economic and material inequality as one of the biggest issues and challenges in modern times. This understanding of inequality refers to the unequal ways in which resources and wealth are distributed across the whole of society with the result that life chances and employment opportunities may also be limited or restricted for many families and children.

Wilkinson and Pickett (2009) provide a cogent and robust argument that it is inequality itself that gives rise to many of our social ills and lack of mobility and that the level of inequality and the level of well-being in any society are inextricably linked. They argue that income inequality is related to deep seated and self-perpetuating processes of social differentiation and observe that countries with much bigger income differences tend to have much lower social mobility.

When considering how inequality operates within society we are faced with the fact that according to the most commonly used measures inequality in the UK is higher than at any time in the last 30 years (Jin et al. 2011). It is clear that being poor and unequal can have negative consequences for all aspects of physical and mental health, but it is a combination of multiple risk factors such as depression of parent, disability, substance abuse, domestic violence and lack of basic skills aggravated by financial stress and housing difficulties that has the highest probability for negative outcomes for children (Sabates and Dex 2012).

Wilkinson and Pickett (2009: 19) collected international data on a range of societal concerns to see whether the occurrence of such problems was greater in unequal societies, including:

- level of trust
- mental illness (including drug and alcohol addiction)

- life expectancy and infant mortality
- obesity
- children's educational performance
- teenage births
- homicides
- imprisonment rates
- social mobility (not available for US states).

They then combined the data to form an Index of Health and Social problems which shows how common these problems are in each country. The evidence was subjected to intensive analysis which clearly showed that in more unequal societies the burden of these problems was much greater. Significantly for the early years sector they then used the Index of Child Well-Being developed by UNICEF (Wilkinson and Pickett 2009: 23) to show the close relationship between child well-being and inequality. They acknowledge the complexity of these interacting issues, especially in terms of material inequality and social hierarchies, saying: 'We should perhaps regard the scale of material inequalities in a society as providing the skeleton, or framework, round which class and cultural differences are formed. Over time, crude differences in wealth gradually become overlaid by differences in clothing, aesthetic taste, education, sense of self and all the other markers of class identity' (Wilkinson and Pickett 2009: 28).

The significance of these assertions should not be underestimated. Importantly, they explode the myth that the amassing of wealth in the developed and developing world automatically means satisfaction and well-being for its citizens. Danny Dorling, a professor of human geography, also raises concerns about the effects of affluence and inequality in education (2010: 32):

> The amassing of riches in affluent countries, the riches which allowed so much to be spent on education, has not resulted in an increased sense of satisfaction in terms of how young people are being taught and are learning. Instead, it has allowed an education system to be created which now express ever increasing anxiety over how pupils perform, in which it has become common to divide up groups of children by so-called ability at younger and younger ages to try to coach them to reach 'appropriate' targets. This has a cumulative effect with adolescents becoming more anxious as a result.

For Dorling, society in general and education in particular, in affluent nations, is underpinned by elitist thinking which has increasingly given rise to the pernicious idea that 'the elite should rule and be differently rewarded because they were most able to rule due to their advanced knowledge and skill rather than because of some feudal tradition' (Dorling 2010: 19). In this way, he argues, elitism has given us a strong reason to justify inequality. Prejudice is not only rife in these societies but also gives rise to the currently prevalent notion that some sectors of society are somehow 'less deserving' because they are not the 'right' kind of human being. Arguably these issues are currently being played out in the UK with a significantly negative effect on outcomes for young children.

Dickins (2013) argues that it is not helpful just to blame families for their perceived shortcomings but that much wider historical, structural, economic and social inequalities are a crucial part of the picture. These must also be examined and addressed if a more cohesive, cooperative and ultimately more equal society is to be achieved and sustained.

Wilkinson and Pickett (2010: 212) acknowledge the evidence of numerous studies which show that the effects of negative early experience can be pivotal and detrimental in later life and go on to suggest that a number of problems directly affecting children, such as poor peer relationships and educational performance, are due to inequality:

> Problems such as these are likely to reflect the way the stresses of a more unequal society – of low social status – have penetrated family life and relationships. Inequality is associated with less good outcomes of many kinds because it leads to a deterioration in the quality of relationships.

The Marmot Review found that almost 60 per cent of five year olds in some of Britain's poorest areas do not reach a 'good level' of behaviour and understanding–double that found in wealthier suburban parts of England (Pordes Bowers et al. 2012). Faced with the body of evidence of inequality in attainment for young children in the UK, the Marmot investigation found that important features of successful engagement with parents included peer support and peer referral; the development of trusting personal relationships between service providers and users; and the provision of a service culture which is responsive to the expressed wishes and needs of parents.

Case study I1

Broad Green is a Wave 2 Sure Start programme, used by over 300 families, which has developed a multi-site facility to deliver the children's centre core offer. The main users are from the Tamil community, followed by White and Black Caribbean. Broad Green has the lowest life expectancy of any of Croydon's wards. Unemployment is higher than for London as a whole. Education and skills deprivation among adults is higher than in the rest of Croydon or in London as a whole. More than half of Broad Green's population is Black minority ethnic.

The centre is highly focused on family support. There are close multi-agency links with health visitors, midwives, child and adolescent mental health services (CAMHS), welfare benefits advisers and Croydon Education Service. The Stay and Play sessions act as a doorway to specialist services on other sites. The programme manager believes in 'a very holistic approach' to family support and sees the play zone as providing the opportunity to 'normalise the concept of providing information, support and advice to parents, within which we have a strategy for vulnerable families'. The main problems which families face are described as language barriers, low self-esteem and confidence, isolation and no social networks.

The centre provides interactive play and language groups, as well as their core offer of health-related workshops, basic skills for parents, volunteering opportunities for parents and family support and outreach. The programme has established a Stay and Play facility. This is open and staffed seven days a week and has a ball pit available to local residents at the weekend. The venue also provides baby clinics and breastfeeding advice.

There is a well-attended father's group which meets independently from the rest of the centre activities on a Saturday morning. There is a monthly Family Support Panel which brings together relevant professionals to 'think together' about what has to be done.

(Adapted from Capacity and Esmee Fairbairn Foundation 2007)

It is often perceived that the least developed countries have the greatest inequality between their citizens, but as Ortiz and Cummins (2011) point out in their report to UNICEF, it is the middle-income countries in which disparities are increasing alarmingly. It is clear that inequality is one of biggest challenges of our time and one which needs to be addressed with some urgency.

Intelligence

In relation to the current debate about the effects of elitism on children's equality of opportunity, it is pertinent to examine some of the thinking underpinning our historical perceptions of children's 'cleverness' and their capacity and ability to succeed within the education system. There is no doubt that negative ideas about children who are considered less intelligent persist within the education system, especially in relation to learning disability.

The work of Charles Darwin on evolution in the early nineteenth century led to widespread scientific interest in the nature of intellect and intelligence. Francis Galton, a cousin of Darwin, studied the lives of a range of eminent or successful people and concluded not only that intelligence was inherited but that intelligence could be seen to follow a pattern of 'natural' distribution; sometimes known as the 'bell curve'.

The bell curve used a theory of distribution which gave rise to the use of terms such as 'percentiles' and 'standard deviations' still referred to today when describing intelligence and for other aspects of development such as weight.

Although Galton did attempt to devise some tests for intelligence, it was Alfred Binet who is usually credited with inventing the first tests which he based on observations of his two daughters. In 1905 Binet and his colleague Theodore Simon devised a series of detailed tests designed to identify children who were in need of remedial teaching. There was a great deal of scientific interest in Galton's work and it was revised and refined by other psychologists of the day including Wilhelm Stern, who in 1912 invented the term 'intelligence quotient', now referred to as IQ. This has been widely used to calculate a person's mental age in relation to their chronological age. Building on Stern's ideas about the measurement of IQ, in 1916 Lewis Terman devised the Stanford-Binet test which, although subject to many adjustments and revisions, still forms the basis for some tests used today.

It is how the tests were used to support ideas about racial and intellectual superiority that gave rise to more sinister developments. Galton's writings are generally considered to have played a key role in launching the eugenic movement in the UK and America. Galton argued that early marriage between healthy, mentally strong families should be encouraged by financial incentives, but that reproduction by the 'feeble-minded' should be curtailed. In his mind, superior mental and physical capabilities were advantageous not only to an individual but also essential for the well-being of society as a whole. Supporters of eugenics believed that governments should support the improvement of the biological 'quality' of the human race through selective parenthood. They thought that physical and learning difficulties were the root cause of a range of social problems including crime, prostitution, alcoholism, vagrancy and unemployment. The eugenics movement, although some believed it was based on a misinterpretation of Darwin's ideas, became very influential and their attitudes and beliefs played a big role in shaping the politics and legislation of the time. Its most extreme manifestation was evident in the policies of Nazi Germany.

Richard Rieser (2002: 27) highlights the influence of this thinking on policy and legislation with the following extract:

> Feeble-minded women are almost invariably immoral and if at large usually become carriers of venereal disease or give birth to children twice as defective as themselves. A feeble-minded woman who marries is twice as prolific as a normal woman ... Every feeble-minded person, especially the high grade imbecile, is a potential criminal needing only the proper environment and opportunity for the development and expression of his criminal tendencies. The unrecognised imbecile is the most dangerous element in society.
>
> (Fernald 1912)

Public statements like the above were used to justify the passing of the 1913 Mental Deficiency Act. The passing of this Act gave rise to the building of many long-stay institutions which tended to be on the outskirts of towns and cities and had the effect of segregating disabled adults and children from the rest of society. Many of the children in such institutions did not receive education as they were considered 'ineducable'. Many of the negative public attitudes that still exist today stem from these policies of segregation which to some degree have been continued by successive governments, although thankfully the long-stay institutions are now closed down.

The 1944 Education Act advocated a selection process to decide which children were deemed 'educable'. For example, children with Down syndrome were considered 'ineducable' until the 1971 Education Act when it was finally officially recognised that no child should be thus labelled and that children with learning disabilities had a legal right to go to school.

No discussion about intelligence is complete without mentioning the work of Howard Gardner whose ideas on 'multiple intelligences' arose from his dissatisfaction with the idea of intelligence as something measurable and concrete enough to be represented by an IQ score. He attempted to define these individual intelligences as follows (Gardner 1993: 33):

- Linguistic intelligence – relating to effective use of language.
- Logical-mathematical intelligence – including problem solving.
- Bodily-kinaesthetic intelligence – concerned with the relationship between the mental and the physical.
- Musical intelligence.
- Spatial intelligence – concerned with the recognition, management and manipulation of wide and confined spaces.
- Naturalistic intelligence – an indication of our evolutionary 'natural' intelligence.
- Intrapersonal intelligence – our understanding of ourselves.

Gardner's work has been very influential and was used by Daniel Goleman (1996) to develop the concept of 'emotional intelligence' whose competencies are manifested in skills and attributes such as self-awareness and empathy.

Although intelligence tests of the sort described earlier are still used in the assessment of children with special educational needs, the simplistic belief that intelligence is only passed down through inheritance has been substantially challenged, especially by those who felt that the tests were subjective and inadequate in the first place. For example, Neo-Marxist theorists such as Bowles and Gintis (1976) regard IQ testing as a mechanism that legitimises inequality and perpetuates social divisions, especially with regard to labour and the workforce. For those who espouse an inclusive approach, it is the causal factors that hinder development, such as poverty and social deprivation, which need to be addressed as a priority. From this perspective, time and effort would be better spent mitigating the effects of disadvantage, rather than undertaking a potentially damaging process of categorisation and subsequent labelling that may in itself be deterministic.

References

Bowles, S. and Gintis, H. (1976) *Schooling in Capitalist America: Education Reform and the Contradiction of Economic Life*. London: Routledge and Kegan Paul.

Capacity and Esmee Fairbairn Foundation (2007) *Children's Centres: Ensuring that Families Most in Need Benefit*. Teddington: Bromgrove Press.

Dickins, M. (2013) Young children's well-being in times of austerity, in J. Manning-Morton (ed.) *Exploring Well-Being in the Early Years*. Maidenhead: Open University Press.

Dorling, D. (2010) *Injustice – Why Social Inequality Persists*. Bristol: The Policy Press.

Fernald, W.E. (1912) The burden of feeble-mindedness, *Journal of Psycho-Asthenics*, 17: 87–111.

Gardner, H. (1993) *Frames of Mind: The Theory of Multiple Intelligences*, 2nd edn. London: Fontana Press.

Goleman, D. (1996) *Emotional Intelligence*. London: Bloomsbury.

Jin, W., Joyce, R., Phillips, D. and Sibieta, L. (2011) *Poverty and Inequality in the UK*. London: Institute for Fiscal Studies.

Ortiz, I. and Cummins, C. (2011) *Global Inequality: Beyond the Bottom Billion*. www.unicef .org/socialpolicy/files/Global_Inequality.pdf (accessed 7 March 2013).

Pordes Bowers, A., Strelitz, J., with Allen, J. and Donkin, A. (2012) *An Equal Start: Improving Outcomes in Children's Centres*. London: UCL Institute of Health Equity.

Rieser, R. (2002) *Disability Equality in Education Course Book*. London: Disability Equality in Education.

Sabates, R. and Dex, S. (2012) *Multiple Risk Factors in Young Children's Development*. London: Centre for longitudinal Studies/Institute of Education.

Wilkinson, R. and Pickett, K. (2009) *The Spirit Level: Why More Equal Societies Almost Always Do Better*. London: Penguin.

J

Joining in

Inclusive practice is all about enabling children to join in all aspects of daily life in a setting regardless of difference. This section aims to explore some of the issues, with a particular focus on play and friendships as areas in which their experiences may be limited by a range of inhibiting external factors such as negative or restrictive attitudes or problems with access to play and learning including physical access.

Photograph J1 Friendships are important

Practice example J1

Stavros, who is four, speaks little English when he arrives at his nursery class. Staff have noticed that he finds it difficult to socialise with other children and join in their games. They make sure that he is not left isolated in free play situations and he gradually becomes more confident in his relationships with other children.

When asked about happy memories of experiences of play, most able-bodied adults talk about pretend games, being in a gang, building dens, playing with mud, playing with water, and so on. Although these responses depend to a certain extent on when they were a child, where they lived and the number of other children around, the list is almost always the same. Micheline Mason (2000), a disabled woman and also a mother of a disabled child, describes a very different experience:

> At first it was not expected that I should live at all, and when that proved to be an unfounded fear, the expectations for me were that I would live all of my life at home with my parents. When I showed a talent for drawing this was heralded as a wonderful thing which meant I could possibly earn a living as a self-employed illustrator working from home. I was considered quite intelligent but this was seen as rather sad, because it meant I would understand how awful my life was to be.
>
> Having a condition which did not improve with physiotherapy or speech therapy, the authorities could see no reason to send me to a special school. However they did not even consider sending me to a mainstream school, because they did not think an ordinary school should be responsible for me. Instead they provided five hours a week home tuition, and the rest of the time I spent alone at home with my mother whilst my able bodied sister went to school just up the road with her friends.
>
> I stayed all day in an empty quiet house drawing. I drew pictures of children playing, children painting, children in fields and on beaches, children at school all together, sitting in little desks just like the one that I sat in at home, on my own. No one asked why. Some days I was so bored and lonely that I would beg my father to take me to work with him. I would hang round his legs as he walked out the front door and he would shake me off onto the doormat, leaving me crying and beating the door with my fists.

Many disabled adults talk about childhoods that were impoverished with respect to play and there is a host of reasons why some children still experience this lack.

Parents may be understandably protective because of negative attitudes or responses to their child's appearance or behaviour. Adults may interpret their roles as doing things for the child rather than being enabling and, not least, adults may be preoccupied by health and safety considerations and the avoidance of risk.

Whereas play should involve challenge, excitement and risk, disabled children are often protected from physical risk, the risk of failure and the possible negative responses of society in general. For most non-disabled children, their most valuable play experiences will involve being with friends with limited adult intervention. Disabled children, on the other hand, will often find themselves restricted to organised group situations such as school or holiday play schemes. They may be in segregated provision or put into groups with other disabled children, and it may be difficult to establish and maintain friendships because of transport problems or the attitude of other parents. They may also be restricted in the range of play experiences they have access to because of low expectations of their potential ability to 'join in' and achieve positive outcomes. Importantly, their primary need to hear language used well in a variety of situations may not have been met particularly if their social experiences have been restricted by isolation or only being with other children who are also experiencing difficulties.

For many disabled children their access to active play and learning may be further restricted by their impairments. Dickins with Denziloe (2003: 13) outline some of the difficulties that children may be experiencing:

- Lack of experience and opportunity can lead to lack of motivation.
- For some children, play may be painful and tiring.
- Children may have experienced failure and feel that if they don't attempt something then at least they can't fail.
- Declining abilities due to a progressive condition can cause children to feel frustrated when they play.
- Children with a sensory impairment, a learning disability or autism may perceive the world as a chaotic and confusing place. This might cause them to withdraw or exhibit behaviour that is stereotypical to their disability or syndrome as a means of understanding, controlling or shutting out the world.
- The intrinsic rewards of play may be limited so the child may need more external rewards such as toys which move, flash with lights, vibrate or make sounds.

Practice example J2

Awa is a three-year-old with severe cerebral palsy and a visual impairment. She uses a specially adapted buggy. She has age appropriate understanding of the world but limited experience of it since her freedom to play, exercise choice and make her own decisions have been limited. Staff at her playgroup wanted to include her in a group painting activity which was taking place on a large sheet of paper on the floor. They hit on the idea of attaching a paintbrush to a sawn off broom handle so that she could reach the floor from her chair. Awa took great pleasure in being able to participate in this activity with the other children and the adaptation was so successful that the non-disabled children wanted an extended brush too.

Caroline Jones (2004: 15) describes a process of 'making exclusion visible' and encourages practitioners to identify physical barriers such as inaccessible buildings, cluttered furniture, hard floors, etc., but also to pay attention to barriers that occur because of negative attitudes. While children will not always be able to participate in all available activities, an inclusive setting should offer all children a real choice of play activities (Ludvigsen et al. 2005).

Friendships are a crucial aspect of the life of all humans beings but for some disabled children they may be more difficult to achieve. Maresa McKeith, who is severely physically disabled and can do little for herself, expresses her difficulty:

> I think that when you don't have friends you can't experience real life because real life is how you get on with other people. I can't do anything on my own so I am completely dependent on people helping me, so if I am not going to be surrounded by only personal assistants, I have got to find a way of making friends.
>
> (McKeith 2000: 8)

Farrell and Scales (1995) undertook a study involving children with severe learning difficulties and children who were not identified as disabled in equal numbers in an inclusive nursery. The children were asked to rank who they would like to play with and sit next to from photographs of all the children in the nursery. Children with severe learning difficulties tended to favour children with or without disabilities equally to play and work with, but children without disabilities showed preference for those without disabilities. However, all of the children with learning difficulties were selected by one or more children without disabilities. The researchers warn that the data was based on hypothetical choices through selection of photographs and might therefore be misleading. They stressed that more accurate data would be obtained by observing children's everyday interactions.

Another study which used direct observations of play in an inclusive nursery (Hanline 1993) found that disabled children interacted with their non-disabled peers

Photograph J2   Can I play with you?

throughout the majority of the observation periods, although disabled children initiated fewer of the interactions. The children did not reject each other and the non-disabled children were tolerant of any difficulties in communication.

It is difficult to draw any definite conclusions as these were all small-scale studies, but they did demonstrate that social interaction can be established at an early age in an inclusive environment. Hunt and Goetz (1997) found through case study analysis of friendships of pupils with severe learning disabilities that where parents of non-disabled children and their teachers were supportive of inclusive education reciprocal friendships were possible.

Research by the children's charity Barnardo's (Ludvigsen et al. 2005: 23) found that 60 play projects in their Better Play programme (91 per cent of those responding to the survey) said that this phrase best described their play provision: 'Disabled children and non-disabled children play together and interact with each other'. When asked how successful they had been in increasing the number of disabled and non-disabled children who played together, 60 per cent of projects described themselves as successful or very successful.

Nutbrown and Clough (2006: 88) use the example of Carter's work on The Playground Buddies Project to show how it was possible to proactively engage children themselves to help peers in various ways, including, playing games, helping lonely children to make friends, or sitting with an unwell child to keep them company.

Children in mainstream settings are more likely to regard themselves as part of their immediate community than children in segregated settings. One reason for this is that special provision is not usually local and children may be picked up by special transport that visibly sets them apart from their peers in the immediate community and can have a stigmatising effect. There are obvious social benefits from having able partners to interact with and positive models for the development of social skills and these are arguably less likely to be found in special provision.

Case study J3

The Markfield Centre in Haringey was established in 1979 by parents of disabled children, whose vision was to create an inclusive place for disabled and non-disabled children to play. Markfield became a charity and limited company in 1983. A Victorian pumphouse in Tottenham was refurbished to create a unique community centre, opened by Diana Princess of Wales in 1986.

Markfield provides a range of services designed to give people access to ordinary and fulfilling life experiences. The centre aims to focus on the whole family with the specific aim of promoting community inclusion, building and strengthening relationships and breaking down isolation and discrimination. Markfield's non-exclusion policy makes it unusual in recognising hidden needs and including people labelled as 'challenging'.

(Adapted from Markfield Project 2013)

Of course disability and impairment are only some of many reasons why certain children might feel discouraged and/or unable to join in and fully participate in the life and learning of a setting. Lane (2008: 23) gives the example of a four-year-old girl who refuses to hold the hand of a child who is Black because she thinks it is 'dirty'. Unless we are carefully observing the social interactions of the children in our care, we are likely to miss opportunities to ensure that every child is fully included.

References

Dickins, M. with Denziloe, J. (2003) *All Together: How to Create Inclusive Services for Disabled Children and their Families*. London: National Children's Bureau.

Farrell, P. and Scales, A. (1995) Who likes to be with whom in an integrated nursery?, *British Journal of Learning Disabilities*, 23: 156–160.

Hanline, M.F. (1993) Inclusion of pre-schoolers with profound disabilities: an analysis of children's interactions, *Journal of the Associations of Persons with Severe Handicaps*, 18: 187–196.

Hunt, P. and Goetz, L. (1997) Research on inclusive educational programmes, practical outcomes for students with severe disabilities, *Journal of Special Education*, 31(1): 3–29.

Jones, C.A. (2004) *Supporting Inclusion in the Early Years*. Maidenhead: Open University Press.

Lane, J. (2008) *Young Children and Racial Justice*. London: National Children's Bureau.

Ludvigsen, A., Creegan, C. and Mills, H. (2005) *Let's Play Together: Play and Inclusion. Evaluation of Better Play Round Three*. Ilford: Barnardo's.

McKeith, M. (2000) *Parents for Inclusion Newsletter*, Spring: p.8.

Markfield Project. www.markfield.org.uk/about-us (accessed 21 March 2013).

Mason, M. (2000) *Incurably Human*. London: Working Press.

Nutbrown, C. and Clough, P. (2006) *Inclusion in the Early Years*. London: Sage.

K

Key person

The concept of a key person approach to working with young children is integral to good inclusive practice because it provides an opportunity for young children to develop a close relationship with someone who not only provides continuity of care but may also lessen any separation anxiety in relation to the parent/child relationship (Elfer et al. 2003; Penn 1999). Central to the idea of a key person approach is the belief that children need a base of loving and secure relationships in order to learn to be strong and independent (DfE 2012).

The terms 'key working' and 'key person' are often used interchangeably but they are very different because the latter is much more concerned with developing trusting and loving attachment relationships than the former, which is more concerned with organisation and strategy. The key person approach is a way of working in which the main focus and organisation of a setting is to support close attachments between individual practitioners and individual children (Roberts 2010). To do this, practitioners need to develop effective key person relationships (Elfer et al. 2003). The evidence suggests that when young children have someone who gets to know them well and supports them with their interaction with others their confidence and sense of well-being is likely to be stronger. Research by Howes et al. (1994) found that young children who felt secure with their 'educarer' displayed complex play with peers and were more gregarious. Children's social competence with peers and their relationship with their practitioner at four years of age were both related to their relationship with their first practitioner.

Selleck (2001) describes clear benefits for the baby or young child as the key person approach ensures that, even given the day-to-day demands of the setting, each child feels special and individual through this close, affectionate, consistent and reliable relationship while they are away from home. Manning-Morton and Thorp (2006: 30) suggest that the role of the key person includes the following:

- The key person shows that they are on the children's side, willing them to succeed and empathising when their early attempts at assertion and negotiation go wrong, acknowledging and verbalising children's good and bad feelings.
- They are able to use important words in each child's home language and are knowledgeable about significant events in the child's cultural and religious life.
- The key person feels confident to talk openly with children about the similarities and differences of ethnicity, gender, ability and family in the group and in the wider community.
- They are able to show fairness by distinguishing between naughtiness and a child's tiredness or misunderstanding and in such situations are able to apply rules flexibly and reasonably.
- They can cope light-heartedly with a toddler's unpredictability and clumsy attempts at assertion because they are interested in working with toddlers, not having power over them.
- Children's efforts are acknowledged and appreciated as well as their achievements so key persons avoid over-using praise and do not give children the message that their efforts are only worthwhile if approved by an adult.

Selleck (2001) observes that the key person approach also has important advantages for parents, as a partnership approach between parent and practitioner who are sharing the pleasures and stresses of an individual child makes it easier to build a strong and trusting relationship with the setting as a whole and the parent is more likely to have peace of mind.

Having a key person should not mean that the child does not build relationships with other members of staff but simply that there is someone in the setting that has them constantly 'in mind' and has the responsibility of supporting them as unique individuals. Elfer et al. (2003: 7–9) summarise the most common objections to implementing the key person approach as follows:

- It brings staff too close to a parental role and they risk becoming overinvolved.
- If children get too close to any one member of staff, it is painful for them if that member of staff is not available.
- It can be threatening to parents who may be jealous of a special relationship between their child and another adult.

- The key person approach is complex to organise and staff need to work as a team, not as individuals.
- It undermines the opportunities for children to participate in all nursery-community relationships.

Elfer et al. (2003) and Manning-Morton and Thorp (2006) point out that although it is appropriate that practitioners keep their professional boundaries intact, this does not mean becoming distant and unavailable. In order to be effective, the key person role needs to be properly understood and supported by the setting management and policies. It is true that this role can be very intense and involves hard work and commitment. However, there can be benefits for the key person in that they really matter to the child and their family.

Practice example K1

Cookham Nursery has been implementing a key person approach for the last two years. Bridget, who is one and a half, attends the nursery and has been diagnosed with Angelman syndrome which has resulted in a delay in her overall development and occasional seizures.

Nisha is Bridget's designated key person at the nursery and prior to her starting she met with Bridget's parents on a home visit and subsequently at the setting. They have discussed and planned a settling in procedure as Bridget tends to get upset when she sees her mother go. As key person, Nisha will be responsible for Bridget's physical care such as changing nappies and administering her medication to prevent seizures.

Nisha has asked her management to provide training on epilepsy for the setting as some practitioners are uneasy about the likelihood of Bridget having a fit. She has established how Bridget likes to be held and handled and what she does when she wants to indicate yes or no. She has also been able to reassure Bridget's parents that if she is unsure about anything relating to Bridget's care she will be sure to contact them as soon as she can. Bridget's parents are really grateful that they have been able to establish a trusting relationship with a staff member from the outset.

Practitioners who have the ability to be sensitive and responsive to their key children can also take pride in the knowledge that they are contributing positively to the child's mental model for future relationships; supporting healthy brain development and contributing to the child's lifelong learning dispositions and abilities.

Photograph K1   Secure and trusting relationships

Knowledge

The saying that 'a little knowledge is a dangerous thing' comes into play here because, although some knowledge is desirable, if it leads to over-generalisation and assumptions about individual children and their families it becomes unhelpful and in some cases positively damaging. For example, the question of how much general medical knowledge of conditions to acquire is a knotty one and brings into play both the medical and the social model of disability. Practitioners often say that they cannot work with disabled children because of their lack of knowledge about impairments, syndromes, conditions, specialised equipment and medical procedures. In fact knowledge about these issues is not a prerequisite. Sometimes it can even be unhelpful and lead to inappropriate limitations being placed on individual children. Most conditions, for example, Down syndrome, cerebral palsy, visual and auditory impairment, will affect individual children in different ways and to different degrees. The danger here is over-generalisation and that too great a focus on medical details obscures the child as an individual and leads to a medical model of disability which views the child as faulty and often neglects the strengths of the child and what they can do.

Practice example K2

Daniel is three and has Down syndrome. He has been attending a local nursery for three half-day sessions. He is settling well but has made it clear that he is unhappy at not being allowed outdoor play with the other children. His mother sets up a meeting with the manager to investigate and it appears that the nursery are under the impression from their knowledge of Down syndrome that he is going to be especially vulnerable to chest complaints. They have been keeping him inside because it is winter. His mother explains that, in fact, he has had minimal problems with his chest and she would much rather he was getting exercise and fresh air and a chance to interact with other children.

If we are working from a social model of disability, what really matters is what an individual child needs us to provide in order for them to achieve quality of life and the opportunity to fulfil their potential. Some general knowledge of a particular impairment or condition may be necessary in order to provide appropriate adaptations and to make adjustments in advance. All children are likely to benefit if we make buildings and learning more accessible. Also it is helpful when working with children on the autistic spectrum, because it enables us to understand that the condition means that a child may be experiencing the world differently to us. However, we should not presume that knowing about a condition or impairment means knowing about an individual child. Micheline Mason (2000: 41) sums up some of the issues raised here:

> It is one of the biggest misconceptions about including children with special needs into schools or communities that people don't have enough 'training'. What they usually mean by this is that they want a formula, designed by 'experts', based on the medical model, which can apply to people with particular impairments or difficulties to make them better. This is the result of the 'professionalising of care'. The last thing anybody thinks is that they can ask the person concerned what help they need and how to give it. If the person has no form of communication then those closest to them can be a great help.

Acquiring knowledge through the internet is not a straightforward process as information on some websites may be inaccurate or may be biased in order to market a particular treatment or approach. The most reliable information will usually come from parents and carers and from careful listening and observations of children themselves. Other professionals such as health visitors and physiotherapists will also have useful information about how best to care for and educate the child. Generally speaking, it is better to acquire knowledge at the point when you need it to support an individual child. You can then build your skills and knowledge through direct experience and by making the child's parents and carers your primary source of information. An additional benefit is that you can also make professional links and build positive relationships with those who are part of the wider team that are caring for a child.

Similarly, misunderstandings can occur when learning about cultures and belief systems. Everyone has an individual culture as a result of their lives and experiences and we must remember that particular faiths can be interpreted in a multitude of different ways. Lane (2008: 117) describes how some books and materials have in the past led to entrenched misconceptions and prejudices. She cites the example of *Child Care and Health for Nursery Nurses*, a book widely recommended during the 1980s which said:

> West Indian children may appear to have a 'different' emotional make-up, and will cry and fight, laugh and love with equal energy. Their responsiveness to music makes it almost impossible for them to remain still when music is being played.... Asian children may appear very passive and dependent on adults, as they are encouraged to be dependent and obedient within their families.
>
> (Brain and Martin 1980: 45)

Such statements are not only misleading but could lead to inappropriate practice around individual children who do not fit these stereotypes. Make sure that any knowledge and information you acquire are from sources which take account of the equality issues raised throughout this book and adhere to the key principles of inclusion.

References

Brain, J. and Martin, M.D. (1980) *Child Care and Health for Nursery Nurses*, 3rd edn. Cheltenham: Nelson Thornes.

Department for Education (DfE, 2012) *Statutory Framework for the Early Years Foundation Stage*. London: HMSO.

Elfer, P., Goldschmied, E. and Selleck, D. (2003) *Key Persons in Nursery: Building Relationships for Quality Provision*. London: David Fulton.

Howes, C., Matheson, C.C. and Hamilton, C.E. (1994) Maternal, teacher, and child care history correlates of children's relationships with peers, *Child Development*, 65: 264–273.

Lane, J. (2008) *Young Children and Racial Justice*. London: National Children's Bureau.

Manning-Morton, J. and Thorp, M. (2006) *Key Times: A Framework for Developing High Quality Provision for Children from Birth to Three Years*. Maidenhead: Open University Press.

Mason, M. (2000) *Incurably Human*. London: Working Press.

Penn, H. (1999) *Early Childhood Services: Theory, Policy and Practice*. Maidenhead: Open University Press.

Roberts, R. (2010) *Well-Being from Birth*. London: Sage.

Selleck, D. (2001) Being under three years of age: enhancing quality experiences, in G. Pugh (ed.) *Contemporary Issues in the Early Years*, 3rd edn. London: Paul Chapman.

L

Legislation for equality

Approaches to equality and inclusion in early years settings are governed by a wider framework of policy and guidance at a national and local level. Legislation plays a key role in determining many aspects of provision for children and families. Legislation, guidance and regulation are constantly evolving and changing to reflect current ideas and opinions about what should be prioritised and what best early years practice should look like. This is therefore a vast and complex area that cannot be thoroughly explored here and the reader is advised to refer to specific guidance for more detail. A lot of the terms used in anti-discriminatory legislation can appear vague to the lay person, such as 'reasonable adjustment' or 'fair treatment'. The process of embedding anti-discriminatory legislation often depends on individuals bringing test cases on one point or another so that a court can interpret and provide clarity on the detail of the law. Thus you will sometimes hear legal professionals refer to 'case law' and/or 'legal precedents' when talking about a particular judgment. It is also important to say that each change to policy and practice has usually been brought about through the struggle and commitment of those groups experiencing prejudice and those who act on their behalf, who have brought these issues to the attention of the general public, media and politicians.

The law currently in place in Great Britain is the Equality Act 2010 which replaces all previous equality legislation. The Act provides a single consolidated source of discrimination law and identifies certain protected characteristics, which are age, disability, gender reassignment, marriage and civil partnership, pregnancy and maternity, race, religion or belief, sex and sexual orientation (Great Britain Parliament 2010). The Act applies to all early years settings, including statutory, voluntary, independent and private provision and childminders. All schools in England, Wales and Scotland, irrespective of how they are funded or managed, have obligations under the Equality Act 2010.

- **Inclusive & anti-discriminatory policies & practices in settings**

- **LA policy**
- **Funding**
- **Training**
- **Support**
- **Regulation**

- **Legislation & political will**
- **Promotion of institutional change**

- **National policy**
- **Funding**
- **Guidance**
- **Support**
- **Regulation**

Figure L1 How we could use the process of inclusion to support equality

The Equality Act covers different kinds of discrimination. Direct discrimination under the Act occurs when someone is treated less favourably or victimised because of a protected characteristic. Indirect discrimination can occur if there is a provision, criterion or practice in place which adversely affects someone with a particular protected characteristic more than others and which cannot be objectively justified as being an appropriate means of achieving a legitimate aim. The Equality Act protects those with protected characteristics from harassment. This refers to bullying and unpleasant behaviour, but potentially extends also to actions which, whether intentionally or unintentionally, cause offence to a person because of a protected characteristic. People who are wrongly perceived of as having a protected characteristic, or those who are associated with someone who has one, are also protected under the law. According to the Equality and Human Rights Commission (EHRC) harassment in schools occurs when someone engages in unwanted behaviour towards a pupil which is related to a relevant protected characteristic and which has the purpose or effect of violating their dignity or creating a hostile, degrading, humiliating or offensive environment for them (EHRC 2013; Lane and Parkes 2012).

The Act introduces protection from discrimination arising from a disability. This is different to direct discrimination and occurs when a person discriminates against an individual because of factors arising from their disability. The reasonable adjustments duty under the Equality Act (Great Britain Parliament 2010) requires providers to avoid as far as possible the disadvantage which a disabled child experiences because of their disability. According to the National Day Nurseries Association (NDNA 2010) the excuse of cost may no longer be an acceptable defence in failing to meet reasonable adjustments.

The Equality Act also introduced a single public sector Equality Duty that applies to all listed public authorities. Under the Act, organisations which are not public authorities but are carrying out public functions are subject to the duty. As the meaning of public functions has been narrowly interpreted this means that voluntary, independent and private settings may not be interpreted as carrying out a public function in their own right. However, the duty unequivocally applies to local authorities, children's centres run by the local authority and maintained nursery schools. It would, however, be good practice for all settings to ensure they follow the principles of the duty. The Act requires those who are subject to the duty to have due regard to the need to eliminate discrimination and any other conduct prohibited by the Act, and to advance equality of opportunity between people who share a protected characteristic and those who do not share it. It also requires them to foster good relations between people who share a protected characteristic and people who do not share it.

There are also relatively new requirements under the new public sector Equality Duty for those listed for specific duties including setting of objectives and publication of equality information that should be taken into account. As part of this process the setting should monitor and evaluate its policy, provision and practice in order to ensure progress.

In addition to legislation specifically concerned with discrimination, there have also been other highly influential pieces of legislation that have impacted on the provision of services for children and families. One of these was the Children Act 1989 which resulted in a major initiative aimed at improving services for children (Great Britain Parliament 1989).

For the first time, the Act included disabled children in the wider framework of legal powers, duties and protections which relate to all children. It stated that every local authority should provide services for disabled children within their area so as to minimise the effect of their disability and it emphasised the need for these children to lead lives which are as normal as possible. It also identified minimum 'fit person' standards for those working with children.

The Children Act 2004 (Great Britain Parliament 2004) further sought to emphasise the importance of inter-agency work and cooperation in meeting the needs of children and to ensure that children's views are ascertained and represented, to improve outcomes for all children, by focusing services more effectively around the needs of children, young people and families. The Act also established the Every Child Matters framework which identified five key outcomes for children which were: being healthy; staying safe; enjoying and achieving; making a positive contribution; and achieving economic well-being.

The Childcare Act 2006 (DfE 2006) placed duties on English local authorities to improve outcomes for young children; to secure sufficient childcare to enable parents to work; and to provide information to parents about childcare and a wide range of services that may be of benefit to them in bringing up their children. The Childcare Act 2006 also placed a duty on local authorities to take into account children's views of the services they receive and this has been influential in promoting the agenda for listening approaches in local authorities and individual settings.

The legislative framework for disability and special education need is covered here in more detail in order to illustrate the policy, processes and procedures required and how they have evolved over time.

The 1981 Education Act (DES 1981) was seminal in that it stated that disabled children should be educated in a mainstream school wherever possible. However, in common with current legislation it allowed significant loopholes including that such placements must be: 'compatible with the best interests of the child'; 'compatible with the interests of the other children'; 'compatible with the efficient use of resources' (Section 316, 1996 Education Act).

It gave local education authorities (Now Children Services Authorities) the duty to assess a child's special educational needs (SEN), to issue a 'statement' of those needs, and to specify the provision that the authority would make to meet them. This was followed by the 1993 Education Act which was eventually incorporated into the Education Act 1996 (DEE 1996). This Act replaced the 1981 Education Act and was designed to address some of the main areas of difficulty stemming from it. It gave greater rights to parents, new duties for schools and firmer procedural rules for the assessment and statementing of children's SEN such as time limits. It still retained the three loopholes, however, brought in with the 1981 Act that effectively limited parental choice.

The original Code of Practice for children with SEN (DfES 2001a) accompanied the 1993 Education Act (now incorporated into the 1996 Act) and provided important guidance and regulations. All settings are required to 'have regard to' the Code of Practice. The Code of Practice currently used (DfES 2001a) was revised alongside legislation in 2001 and is currently under further review.

Although the Disability Discrimination Act (Great Britain Parliament 1995) has been now replaced by the Equality Act 2010, which has made the notion of discrimination arising from disability more explicit, it was historically important in that it brought in legal measures to clarify disabled people's rights in terms of employment, obtaining goods and services and buying or renting land or property. It meant that early years providers had a duty not to discriminate against disabled pupils in education, day care or other services within their provision. At the time the DDA set out two main duties:

1. Not to treat a disabled child 'less favourably', for example, excluding children from activities or outings without attempting to make them accessible.
2. To make 'reasonable adjustments' for disabled children, for example, planning ahead to ensure that all aspects of policy and planning are not discriminatory.

This was followed by the Special Educational Needs and Disability Act (DfES 2001b), which effectively implemented aspects of the DDA in schools and required schools and local education authorities (LEAs) to develop accessibility plans and strategies and to look at how they could best build this planning into individual service and authority-wide planning structures. This Act changed the conditions in the 1996 Act that limited the LEA's duty to provide a mainstream school place for a child with SEN and required schools to inform parents when they make special education provision because they have identified their child as having SEN. This meant, however, that provision for disabled children still had to be 'compatible with the interests of the other children'.

Now a new Children and Families Bill is making its way through the parliamentary process which contains many of the recommendations set out in the Green Paper and consultation *Support and Aspiration: A New Approach to Special Educational Needs and Disability* (DfE 2012b) which was introduced to Parliament in early 2013 with implementation planned from spring 2014. This Bill promises earlier identification and support and an increase in control and choice for parents regarding their child's provision.

Also part of the evolving picture is the new *Early Years Foundation Stage* (EYFS) document (DfE 2012a) with revised Early Learning Goals with an emphasis on school readiness, and for two year olds a progress check and expanded provision for those deemed to be disadvantaged. The statutory framework of the EYFS 2012 applies to England only.

Although it is not a requirement, some early years settings, as part of good practice, have set up a Single Equality Scheme that covers the main recommended areas of possible discrimination. Useful questions for providers to ask themselves when developing a policy are as follows:

- When were your policies last updated and how often are they reviewed?
- Are they up to date in view of current legislative requirements?
- How are your policies disseminated to parents and staff?
- Do you think that your policies are effective in helping you to work towards inclusive practice?

It is important that all providers in the early years stay abreast of the relevant legislation and guidance, but also to remember that these are usually minimum standards which can be significantly improved upon.

Listening to children

Listening to young children and babies is a key aspect of inclusive practice because it helps to ensure that they feel valued and respected and provided for in a caring, appropriate and attentive fashion. It can make an enormous difference to how young children feel about themselves as well as helping practitioners by providing insights into children's priorities, interests and concerns. Through being listened to we learn many essential skills such as listening, debating, negotiating and compromising. We develop a deeper sense of the needs of others, an increased sense of ownership and responsibility for where we live, play and learn, and we learn whether or not we have a voice that is worth listening to. Importantly it can also form a useful strand of any assessment process.

Article 12 of the United Nations Convention on the Rights of the Child (UNCRC) states that children have a right to say what they think about anything that affects them and must be listened to carefully. Courts and official bodies must also listen to children's viewpoints when making decisions which affect them. In England and Wales, the Childcare Act 2006 (DfE 2006) placed a duty on local authorities to take into account children's views of the services they receive

This aspect of practice is extremely variable: with some settings using listening as part of their ordinary everyday practice; some consulting on particular issues and not on others; and some settings for whom this may be an aspect of practice which they have not yet considered. The goal of improving practice in this area should be the establishment of a 'culture' of listening throughout the setting. A listening culture has been described by Williams (2011: 1) as 'one in which listening to individual experiences and views is identified as a core feature of the setting approach and ethos'.

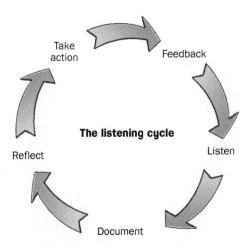

Figure L2 The listening cycle (adapted from McAuliffe 2003)

Integral to these processes is the ideal of a listening cycle that includes a process of listening, documenting, reflecting, taking action and feedback. This is important because listening without action and reflection can be interpreted as a lack of respect for those who are being consulted. Imagine if a manager carefully consulted staff about shift changes or role changes and then completely ignored what had been said. Feedback is really important because, even if it is not possible to take on recommendations, staff need to know that their suggestions have been valued and the reasons why they could not be taken up. In order to be effective, any consultation should reflect and record all these aspects of the listening cycle.

Alison Clark (2011: 1) defines listening as: 'an active process of receiving (hearing and observing) interpreting and responding to communication. It includes all of the senses and emotions and is not limited to the spoken word'. It can involve painting, drama, photographs, sensory walks and a host of other activities. It is not just about receiving information but about how we interpret and respond to it as well. Sensitive use of observation strategies may also be necessary in order to really tune in to what children are communicating to us. According to Clark (2011: 5), how we listen to young children will depend on why we are listening:

- to tune into children as part of their everyday lives
- to listen as part of a specific consultation about a particular entitlement, choice, event or opportunity
- to find out about their thoughts and feelings.

In addition to vocalisation, the use of facial expressions, body language and gesture are all important ways in which babies and young children communicate long before the emergence of language. For example, it is useful for us to remember that although a baby's crying makes us tense and uncomfortable, this discomfort propels us into action, which is what the baby needs (Goldschmied and Jackson 1994). This in itself can be regarded as a conversation and an early experience of cause and effect for the baby (Gopnik et al. 1999).

Acredolo and Goodwyn (2000) suggest that all babies use signs and gestures such as pointing, waving goodbye, nodding and shaking their heads. Their research (Acredolo and Goodwyn 1985) identified that where babies were supported in using signs to communicate their needs they had more spoken language at two years old than non-signing peers. Young children in their study also experienced less frustration as signing enabled them to communicate more effectively with their parents/carers, thus enhancing their relationships.

Lancaster (2010) makes a compelling case for listening to young children in the context of the UNCRC and Every Child Matters and describes the development of listening practice in recent years. She makes the point that an emphasis on children engaging in decision-making processes raises their status to stakeholder rather than passive recipients of service provision. For example, Lancaster (2010: 84) describes how young children were involved in staff recruitment. In some local authority areas these processes have become so embedded that young children's voices are enabled to be heard systematically on a whole range of wider issues.

The 'mosaic approach' (Clark and Moss 2001: 5) has been widely used in settings to consult children on a variety of issues. This approach is successful because, as the authors point out, it incorporates a number of factors:

- **Multi-method**: recognises the different 'voices' or languages of children.
- **Participatory**: treats children as experts and agents in their own lives.
- **Reflexive**: includes children, practitioners and parents in reflecting on meanings; addresses the question of interpretation.
- **Adaptable**: can be applied in a variety of early childhood institutions.
- **Focused on children's lived experiences**: can be used for a variety of purposes including looking at lives lived rather than knowledge gained or care received.
- **Embedded into practice**: a framework for listening which has the potential to be used both as an evaluative tool and to become embedded into early years practice.

Case study L1

Save the Children and the Children's Society worked with practitioners and children in early years settings in London. Their aim was to gain an insight into young children's perceptions of their environment to demonstrate to London regional government that young children have views on improving London. The exercise successfully demonstrated that, if 'listened to' in the appropriate way, children do have opinions on wider issues that should be taken into account by service planners.

The children, aged between two-and-a-half and four years, went on a 'sensory walk' of their neighbourhoods. Practitioners noted children's comments and reflections and, as they walked, children also took photographs of their surroundings. Children then came back into their settings and drew pictures and discussed what they had seen.

The collected views enabled adults to understand what London is like from the perspective of a young child. In particular the photographs illustrated that issues such as rubbish on the streets, car exhaust fumes, crossing roads between parked cars and dirty parks fouled by dogs have a great impact on young children's experience of life in the city. Children also talked about the environments they like. Their words and pictures were made into a leaflet and presented to a representative of the Mayor of London. (McLarnon and Emerson 2002).

The 'listening' agenda has sometimes been criticised on ethical grounds because of the power and influence adults may have over children and because they are seen as easily manipulated. The following guidelines for ethical practice should help to offset any potential ethical difficulties:

- Be clear as to why you are consulting children and for what purpose.
- Know how the information gained will be used and processed.
- Methods used must be truly participatory, enjoyable and negotiable.
- Children should not be forced to participate – respect their right to say no.
- Show genuine respect for the child.
- Listen carefully to their views and check out that you have understood what they want to say – do not interpret for them.
- Provide the right amount of information, in a form they can understand, to help them make a response.

Whilst emphasising the importance of listening, Brooker (2011: 140) makes the point that the power hierarchy in settings can interfere with this process. If practitioners think they know best, then they are more likely to relegate their 'listening' to trivial matters. She adds: 'Listening that is tokenistic may further reinforce the power and status difference between the listener and the listened to'.

Photograph L1 A chance to listen and share stories

Whatever the pitfalls, in terms of inclusion listening is integral to good practice. As Peter Moss (2001: 16) points out:

> Listening is not only a complex concept, but it goes to the heart of the theories, relationships and practice that shape early childhood work. It should not be an add-on, to meet some external requirement . . . if we choose to listen to young children, it should be because listening is part of our beliefs about learning, relationships, democracy and ethics. It is an integral part of how we think life should be lived.

Case study L2

In order to develop their 'Listening to Young Children Strategy' Newcastle local authority established a network of Children's Champions to share good practice and information about participation work with young children. To support this process a listening to young children officer (LTYCO) was also appointed to work directly with practitioners by providing a range of training opportunities and peer support networks. From the onset it was agreed that in order to empower young children to participate in democratic processes the qualities of listening to young children would need to be embedded as a way of life within the workforce.

The LTYCO works directly with staff teams within settings to embed good practice, challenge myths and develop an ethos of listening. During training workshops, teams are encouraged to take a solution-focused approach and to work collaboratively. They are thus able to identify and celebrate areas of success, identify gaps and discuss realistic solutions to barriers.

The whole team is encouraged to adopt collective responsibility for listening whilst recognising individual responsibilities and strengths. In this way the ownership of listening to children becomes unique to each setting and embedded as a natural process. As staff 'tune in' to young children, a culture of consultation and change can be established which promotes confidence and raises the self-esteem of all of those involved. The local authority aims to develop a sensitive listening partnership with children, their families and practitioners. Through practitioner network meetings the Children's Champions then discuss, explore and review consultation methodology with a view to improving opportunities for children to influence change as it takes place across the locality.

(Adapted from Dickins 2011)

There may also be attitudinal and cultural barriers to identify and overcome. Each setting is likely to face individual challenges. In the process of embedding a listening culture team, members may need to consider how specific issues such as prejudice and discrimination may be impacting on the accessibility and quality of their service in terms of the experience of children and families and individual team members. Access to appropriate training and support, opportunities for honest personal and professional reflection, support for staff to find the language they feel comfortable with so they can listen and respond with confidence, and the celebration and sharing of positive practice will all help to underpin this process.

References

Acredolo L. and Goodwyn, S. (1985) Symbolic gesturing in language development: a case study, *Human Development*, 28: 40–49.

Acredolo, L. and Goodwyn, S. (2000) *Baby Signs. How to Talk with your Baby before your Baby Can Talk*. London: Ebury Press.

Brooker, L. (2011) Taking children seriously: an alternative agenda for research? *Journal of Early Childhood Research*, 9(2): 137–149.

Clark, A. (2011) *Listening as a Way of Life: Why and How We Listen to Young Children*. London: National Children's Bureau.

Clark, A. and Moss, P. (2001) *Listening To Young Children: The Mosaic Approach*. London: National Children's Bureau.

Department for Education (DfE 2006) *Childcare Act 2006*. London: HMSO.

Department for Education (DfE, 2012a) *Early Years Foundation Stage (revised)*. www.foundationyears.org.uk/early-years-foundation-stage-2012/ (accessed 13 March 2013).

Department for Education (DfE, 2012b) *Support and Aspiration: A New Approach to Special Educational Needs and Disability: Progress and Next Steps*. London: HMSO.

Department for Education and Skills (DfES, 2001a) *Special Education Needs: Code of Practice*. Nottingham: DfES.

Department for Education and Skills (DfES, 2001b) *Special Educational Needs and Disability Act*. London: HMSO.

Department of Education and Science (DES, 1981) *Education Act*. London: HMSO.

Dickins, M. (2011) *Listening as a Way of Life: Leadership for Listening*. London: National Children's Bureau.

Disability Equality in Education (DEE, 1996) *Education Act 1996: Part IV, Special Educational Needs*. London: HMSO.

Equality and Human Rights Commission (EHRC 2013) *Harassment*. http://www.equalityhumanrights.com/advice-and-guidance/education-providers-schools-guidance/key-concepts/harassment/ (accessed 27 September 2013).

Goldschmied, E. and Jackson, S. (1994) *People Under Three: Young Children in Day Care*. London: Routledge.

Gopnik, A., Meltzoff, A. and Kuhl, P. (1999) *How Babies Think*. London: Weidenfield and Nicolson.

Great Britain Parliament (1989) *Children Act 1989*. London: HMSO.

Great Britain Parliament (1995) *Disability Discrimination Act (DDA) 1995*. London: HMSO.

Great Britain Parliament (2004) *Children Act 2004.* London: HMSO.

Great Britain Parliament (2010) *Equality Act 2010.* London: HMSO.

Lancaster, Y.P. (2010) Listening to young children: enabling children to be seen and heard, in Pugh, G. and Duffy, B. (2010) *Contemporary Issues in Early Years,* 5th edn. London: Sage.

Lane, J. and Parkes, B. (2012) The Equality Act 2010 – acting to end discrimination, *Nursery World/Nursery Management,* 19 March.

McAuliffe, A. (2003) *When are We having Candy-floss? Report on a Project to Investigate Consultation with Very Young Children in Early Years Services.* London: National Children's Bureau.

McLarnon, J. and Emerson, S. (2002) *London on your Doorstep.* London: The Children's Society and Save the Children.

Moss, P. (2001) All about consulting with children, *Nursery World,* 5 July.

National Day Nurseries Association (2010) *Member Factsheet: Equality Act 2010.* http://www.ndna.org.uk/Resources/NDNA/Public%20Factsheets/027%20Equality%20Act%20factsheet%20(Nov%2010).pdf (accessed 27 September 2013).

Williams, L. (2011) *Listening as a Way of Life: Developing a Listening Culture.* London: National Children's Bureau.

M

Management and leadership
Mixed heritage

Management and leadership

Although management and leadership are linked and often interdependent they should not be seen as synonymous. Schon (1983) observes that an individual can fulfil many of the conditions usually associated with leadership, for example, being inspirational, a symbol, an educator and so on, without carrying any of the responsibilities of formal management. Similarly, we will all have known individuals who may have appeared to be efficient in terms of the nuts and bolts of day-to-day management but who failed to inspire and were even resistant to positive change. Rodd (2005: 23) makes this point:

> A person with highly developed management skills is likely to have structured the administration of the program to give adequate time to key leadership functions. A person with poorly developed management skills is unlikely to be sufficiently organised to free up the time needed to focus on leadership issues. In any case management skills are necessary but not sufficient for effective leadership.

Dickins (2011) argues that a distributive and consultative model of leadership is the best for supporting and developing inclusive practice. In this context leadership is regarded as a broad role rather than a limited function, and one which can be simultaneously fulfilled by several people. Jones and Pound (2008: 10) suggest that persons in a managerial role should be viewed as a 'leader of leaders' and suggest a broader concept of leadership in early years settings in order to create a culture of 'inclusive leadership' in which each individual is encouraged to see themselves as a potential leader in some aspect of their practice.

Although a distinction is made here between the two sets of skills, it is still recognised that in terms of day-to-day practice they may often be overlapping, interdependent and entwined. These issues deserve our attention because the management and leadership of an early years setting has been found to be crucial to the establishment of inclusive principles and the embedding of inclusive practice. (Ofsted 2005; Moyles 2006)

Many attempts have been made over the years to categorise management functions. Although there are variations between different versions, most of them would include planning and organisation, motivation and communication as well as problem solving and evaluation. All of these functions are central to the general organisation of any early years provision, but they are also integral to the promotion and development of inclusive practice which should inevitably involve changes in policy practice and procedures. While management is required to keep a provision running efficiently, leadership is more concerned with getting the best that is possible. Effective leadership should entail engagement with all aspects of policy and practice in order to inspire and motivate others, in the best interests of the children and their families.

Dickins (2011: 1) uses the following definition of leadership in relation to a listening culture within settings that has resonance here. Whilst acknowledging the many different professional understandings of leadership, from this perspective it is defined as: 'an enabling process through which individuals can inspire, articulate, influence and implement a shared, collective vision of principles, policy and practice'. This definition is useful in relation to inclusion as it places the development of shared values and positive relationships between staff, parents and children at the heart of the process. Jones and Pound (2008: 10) refer to the culture of 'inclusive' leadership:

> The move away from the idea that leadership is the exclusive preserve of one person to a process of sharing professional knowledge, skills and personalities, combining and reflecting, striving for continuous improvement, suggests that the actions of every member of the early years team impact on the quality of the provision.

Solly (2003, cited in Rodd 2005: 21) argues that supporting the development of relationships between all of the members of early childhood communities and teamwork are vital if leadership in early childhood settings is to be effective: 'Leadership emanates out of vision that is based in philosophy, values and beliefs, which in turn guides policy, day-to-day operation and innovation. It is manifested through strategic planning that grows out of reflection'.

To some degree all members of staff are required to be both managers and leaders as they too are likely to be concerned with and engaged in all of the management functions previously described. The seniority and place within the power structure of managers, however, means that even small changes to practice can be difficult to effect unless the manager is on board.

Practice example M1

At Wenlock Nursery the team has prioritised the development and strengthening of relationships between practitioners, children and their families. They see it as important that the views and values of all partners are reflected in policy and practice.

Part of this process has involved the development of systems to record, analyse and resource children's learning needs through the collection of information. The current manager has linked this to the developing leadership role of practitioners to reflect the supportive nature of their posts as key persons to a named group of children and their families.

At Wenlock there is a value system that treats experience as more important than qualifications or status alone. Less qualified staff are also motivated and encouraged to take on a leadership role even if they have never perceived themselves as leaders.

Mutual trust is seen as fundamental to effective collaborative leadership and daily interaction and communication is considered essential to the process. The role of management at Wenlock is seen as overarching but not controlling.

A report from the National Federation for Educational Research (NFER, Martin et al. 2009: iv–v) set out to identify those leadership qualities and functions which were most effective in narrowing the gap in outcomes between vulnerable children and young people. They found that the gap appears to be narrowed through leadership in local authorities at all levels, which emphasises the following:

- Prioritising the most vulnerable and developing a local vision.
- Championing the voice of vulnerable groups and encouraging their participation.
- Using good quality data to identify needs and provide services for vulnerable groups; collecting 'real time' intelligence on emerging needs; gathering information directly from children, young people and their families and the local community.
- Fostering partnership working around vulnerable groups; being committed to joint working which focuses on the most vulnerable.
- Developing and motivating the workforce to improve outcomes for vulnerable groups.
- Having an unrelenting drive and passion to improve outcomes for vulnerable groups; having a genuine empathy and commitment to support the most vulnerable; instilling a 'can-do ethos' and the expectation that the vision will be delivered.

In writing about leadership, Moyles (2006: 53) points out:

> Values are not shared if the head sits in her office, looking down on her staff, telling them constantly what they should do and how they should do it. Values are only 'shared' if they have arisen organically from staff and management, through talking and reflecting on experience.

The implication here is that effective and inclusive leadership should be proactive with a strong democratic emphasis on involving and sharing power with other people rather than autocratic and remote.

Mixed heritage

The term 'mixed heritage' is used here to refer to children and families with mixed race or ethnicity. According to data released from the Office for National Statistics (Rogers 2011) The mixed race population in the UK is up nearly 50 per cent to almost a million for the first time – up from 672,000 in 2001 to 986,600 in 2009. A third of those identified are mixed African-Caribbean and White, followed by Asian/White. These figures confirm that there is a growing population of children and families for whom the issue of identity may be less than straightforward, though not necessarily problematic in itself.

Lane (2008: 191) points out that nearly all of us belong to mixed backgrounds of one sort or another, but that for some children the visible differences between their parents are more apparent than others and the issues of how they define themselves and in turn are defined by others becomes central to the already complex process of identity formation. Commentators such as Yasmin Alibhai-Brown have expressed the major worry that many organisations and institutions in Britain have been influenced by the United States. In a BBC interview she points out:

> The movement started there to claim all mixed race children as black – the argument was if they suffer racism nobody asks them if they're mixed race. But I think big mistakes were made to drive policy makers and practitioners into accepting this rather ludicrous concept because mixed race children aren't black and they're not white or brown – they are themselves. (Alibhai-Brown 2002)

One of the most influential UK studies in this area was conducted by Anne Wilson in 1987. Wilson's research was focused on children of White/Black parentage and its major purpose was to discover whether 'mixed race' children were 'misfits' stranded between identities, as was widely believed at the time. Wilson found that most of the children in the study did express a positive identity and did not find a conflict in having a mixed heritage. This was especially found to be true if their mothers saw them as mixed or Black and were secure about their own position (Wilson 1987). Wilson also found that the outcomes were most positive where race was discussed openly and honestly within families and schools, and when families live in multi-racial areas.

In the early 1990s research on this area of identity was carried out by Barbara Tizzard and Ann Phoenix who interviewed 15 to 16 year olds of both sexes and from a range of backgrounds and circumstances (Tizzard and Phoenix 1993). The conclusion they reached from this research was that a significant proportion of the young people interviewed rejected the idea that they should see themselves as Black and felt that to do so would be to deny their White heritage. Those who did define themselves as Black tended to be more politicised and saw their oppression by White people and their experiences of racism as important and influential factors in their lives. The researchers also found that family dynamics had a far greater influence on the identities of those in the study than the schools they attended. However, the complexities of the issue were something they were keen to acknowledge, as was the variety and range of opinions they encountered.

Alibhai-Brown (2001) highlights evidence from US studies (Taylor Gibbs and Hines 1992) which found that a higher socio-ecnomic status and integrated schooling in a mixed neighbourhood produced the best adjusted young people, but also found that where families had confronted the issue of their mixed race identity the outcomes for the children were likely to be better. Research in the UK into the educational needs of mixed race pupils was conducted by Tickly et al. (2004) whose key findings included that the attainment of White/Black Caribbean pupils is below average, while the attainment of White/Black African pupils is similar to average in primary schools and slightly below average in secondary schools. The attainment of White/Asian pupils, however, is above average. They also found:

> The key barriers to achievement facing pupils of White/Black Caribbean origin are in many cases similar to those faced by pupils of Black Caribbean origin. They are more likely to come from socially disadvantaged backgrounds; are more likely to experience forms of institutionalised racism in the form of low teacher expectations; and, are more likely to be excluded from school. White/Black Caribbean pupils also face specific barriers to achievement.
>
> (Tickly et al. 2004: 6)

Tickly observes that low expectations of pupils by teachers often seem based on a stereotypical view of the fragmented home backgrounds and 'confused' identities of White/Black Caribbean pupils. These pupils often experience racism from teachers and from their White and Black peers targeted at their mixed heritage. This can lead to the adoption of what are perceived to be rebellious and challenging forms of behaviour. The barriers to achievement experienced by White/Black Caribbean pupils operate in a context where mixed heritage identities (including those of

White/Black Caribbean, White/Black African and White/Asian pupils) are not recognised in the curriculum or in policies of schools and of children's services authorities (CSA) formely LEAs. In the case of White/Black Caribbean pupils, their invisibility from policy makes it difficult for their underachievement to be challenged. In those schools where White/Black Caribbean pupils achieve relatively highly they often benefit from inclusion in policies targeted at Black Caribbean learners, with whom they share similar barriers to achievement and with whom they often identify. Even in these schools, however, the specific barriers to achievement faced by White/Black Caribbean learners are rarely explicitly addressed.

Practice example M2

Four-year-old Akua has a mixed heritage as her mother is White British and her father who is Black is from Ghana. Akua's own skin tone is white although that of her younger sibling Kwami is much darker. Staff at the nursery were at first confused since they had not met the children's father and assumed that the children must have different fathers. Issues had also arisen because Akua's mother reported that Akua had been teased by another child because of the difference in appearance between her and her brother. Akua's key worker Patrice decided to take on this issue and sourced books and images that reflected families with a mixed heritage. She raised the issue at a staff meeting to ensure that everyone was aware of the family identity. She also used a Persona Doll as a means of discussing with the children how mothers and fathers can be different.

Many of the issues identified above have resonance and implications for inclusive early years practice. Lane (2008) recommends that multiple and mixed identities should be affirmed and treated as the norm with all children and their families and that children having more than one culture in their family should be helped to feel proud of both or all of their cultures. Importantly, instead of making assumptions, we should be listening to individual children and families about how they feel and wish to be identified and ensuring that our policies, principles and practice encourage a positive identity and sense of selfe-steem to develop.

References

Alibhai-Brown, Y. (2001) *Mixed Feelings: The Complex Lives of Mixed-Race Britons*. London: Women's Press.

Alibhai-Brown, Y. (2002) *Changing Face of Britain*. http://news.bbc.co.uk/hi/english/static/in_depth/uk/2002/race/changing_face_of_britain.stm (accessed 18 March 2013).

Dickins, M. (2011) *Listening as a Way of Life: Leadership for Listening*. London: National Children's Bureau.

Jones, A. and Pound, L. (2008) *Leadership and Management in the Early Years: From Principles to Practice*. Maidenhead: Open University Press.

Lane, J. (2008) *Young Children and Racial Justice*. London: National Children's Bureau.

Martin, K., Lord, P., White, R. and Atkinson, M. (2009) *Narrowing the Gap in Outcomes: Leadership (LGA Research Report)*. Slough: National Foundation for Educational Research.

Moyles, J. (2006) *Effective Leadership and Management in the Early Years*. Maidenhead: Open University Press.

Ofsted (2005) *Removing Barriers: A 'Can-do' Approach*. London: Manchester Ofsted.

Rodd, J. (2005) *Leadership in Early Childhood*. Maidenhead: Open University Press.

Rogers, S. (2011) Non–white British population reaches 9.1 million. www.guardian.co.uk/society/2011/may/18/non-white-british-population-ons (accessed 18 March 2013).

Schon, D. (1983) *The Reflective Practitioner: How Professionals Think in Action*. New York: Basic Books.

Taylor Gibbs, J. and Hines, A.M. (1992) Negotiating ethnic identity: issues for black–white biracial adults, in M. Root, *Racially Mixed People in America*. Newbury Park, CA: Sage.

Tickly, L., Caballero, C., Haynes, J. and Hill, J. (2004) *Understanding the Educational Needs of Mixed Heritage Pupils*. Bristol: University of Bristol.

Tizzard, B. and Phoenix, A. (1993) *Black, White or Mixed Race*. London: Routledge.

Wilson, A. (1987) *Mixed Race Children: A Study of Identity*. London: Allen and Unwin.

N

Negotiation and conflict resolution

If we think about inclusion as a process of identifying and overcoming barriers, it becomes obvious that some conflicts may arise as part of negotiating the necessary changes and adjustment to provision and practice. The process of building a shared vision and values may also present difficulties and challenges within teams and for individuals whose life experience, belief systems and culture may be quite different. This section explores the skills necessary for negotiation and conflict management in the context of managing change in early years settings. Rodd (1994: 104) observes:

> Conflict in its various forms appears to be a constant feature of the psychological climate of early childhood services, given the frequency and intensity of disagreements, arguments, quarrels and disputes which are reported by practitioners, managers and leaders.

Rodd attributes this to the very nature of the early childhood context whereby staff and parents with individual and competing philosophies, values, belief systems and understandings endeavour to work together in the best interests of young children. Although prolonged conflict can be very harmful, Rodd also identifies a positive role and function in providing opportunity and motivation for learning and growth. She stresses that it is how conflicts are managed that will be pivotal in terms of a positive or negative outcome.

Negotiation skills will be necessary in order to achieve effective compromise and resolution in any given situation. Effective negotiators will need the skills to analyse a problem, first identifying the issue, taking into account the differing perspectives as well as the desired outcome goal. They need to be well prepared and to listen actively to all parties, whilst communicating effectively themselves. Effective negotiators will also foster a collaborative non-combative team approach and be able to act decisively when required.

Siraj-Blatchford and Manni (2007: 17) found that effective leaders accept the inevitability of change and embrace it. They are able to plan for change and manage it so that everyone feels part of the process:

> Any resistance to change appeared to be overcome by the development of a climate and culture for change that was established through the routine collaborative review of current practice and policy. These routines of review validated the processes of change, promoting confidence and acceptance where there might have been fear or resistance.

They stress that staff should be enabled to regard change as emerging out of real needs that they themselves have observed and experienced rather than as externally imposed just for the sake of change. They see effective leaders as 'reflective practitioners who influence and develop people by setting an example and providing a model, both morally and purposefully' (Siraj-Blatchford and Manni 2007: 22).

Plant (1987) suggests that resistance to change often comes in systemic and behavioural forms. Systemic resistance tends to occur when the change is perceived of as difficult, not considered feasible, or as poorly underpinned by knowledge, information, skill and managerial capacity. By contrast, behavioural resistance is more emotionally centred and derives from the reactions, perceptions and assumptions of individuals and/or the organisation involved.

Coulson (1985) has provided a valuable insight into the psychology of change which offers guidance to managers as they contemplate the way forward. First, initiators of the management of change need to be aware that when change is suggested those involved in it want to protect what they see themselves to be. Second, they need to recognise that staff strive to satisfy their own work needs and the expectations of others with the minimum of uncertainty and anxiety. Pressure to alter this way of being tends to be received as threatening to their comfortable continuity of living and working. Third, suggestions that individuals change their way of doing things and their approaches to the professional tasks for which they have responsibility implies a level of inadequacy in their performance, and this must be recognised. All these factors can threaten the identity that staff have striven to develop and they need to be anticipated, understood and taken into account. Far too often managers and senior staff experience a defensive tendency as opposition to new ideas and see their task as one of overcoming the perceived resistance. An approach that recognises the strengths of existing practice and the positive qualities of an individual will be most effective when addressing weaknesses.

Rodd (1994) describes how prolonged conflict and power struggles can diminish team productivity and lead to members becoming 'stuck' in a 'destructive cycle of discord'. She argues that listening and communication are central to successful strategies, as are attention to staff morale, self-esteem and confidence.

Moyles (2006: 122) usefully highlights the qualities that leaders should aspire to in relation to conflict resolution, but they could equally well apply to any individual seeking to achieve an equitable and constructive solution to a conflict or dispute. These have been summarised below and echo much of what has already been high-lighted in this section:

- Be receptive to suggestions and develop opportunities to hear them.
- Negotiate, respect and utilise different viewpoints.
- Listen actively to staff and parents and undertake the necessary mediation.
- Listen actively to children – including inarticulate messages.
- Resolve tensions between individuals and understand compromise.
- Be capable of identifying, resolving and, where relevant, averting conflict.
- Understand internal conflicts and view them as inevitable or even necessary.
- Take a calm, positive and tolerant approach to conflicts and crises.

Practice example N1

Gayle has been appointed as a special educational needs coordinator (SENCo) at her nursery setting and has decided to tackle the issue of how lunchtimes are organised at her setting. Currently there are three disabled children attending who have physical difficulty with feeding themselves who are required to have their lunch in a separate room. Gayle is not only concerned about the negative messages this might be giving the children concerned but also about the effect of this practice on the non-disabled children as it enhances and accentuates the differences between them. When she raises this at a staff meeting some mem-bers of staff react with outrage saying that the children are much too 'messy' and they want children to learn and to model good 'table manners'. The centre manager is generally supportive of the issue but concerned at the conflict that is developing.

In her capacity as SENCo Gayle listens carefully to the viewpoint of each of the practitioners and concludes that there is a lack of basic understanding about inclusive practice and why it is important and some fear and trepidation about the physical care required by the disabled children. She contacts a local disability charity and arranges for an inset training day on disability equality issues and inclusive practice. She also conducts a good practice audit so that she can highlight to staff that she values their efforts and what they are doing well already. Eventually a compromise is reached that all the children will eat together once a week as a trial. After a few weeks, when none of the anticipated difficulties arise and they have had the opportunity to get to know the children better, staff withdraw their objections and the practice is adopted as part of everyday routine.

Sensitive conflict resolution and negotiation are at the heart of inclusive practice. A dysfunctional, dissatisfied and resentful team is much less likely to be able to develop a tolerant and empathetic ethos in their work with children and families.

Networking

Networking is all about building mutually beneficial relationships and talking to people with a view to discussing topics and issues that are of joint interest. Effective inclusive practice can be hard to achieve in isolation and talking to others can stimulate creativity and awareness of other ways of achieving goals and improving outcomes for staff, children and families. All of the stakeholders involved in early years provision can therefore benefit from opportunities to network with others in a similar role or situation. In the context of developing and implementing inclusive practice, networks are important, especially when changes are being implemented.

It is useful to think of networks as interconnected systems of people which can serve a number of functions for their members, including the opportunity to share knowledge, policy, information and experiences; compare and contrast current practice; and to highlight and address overarching problems and issues. Networks can also provide a collective voice for individuals and groups that might otherwise have been ignored.

Examples of networks that operate nationally (England) include the National Quality Improvement Network (NQIN) convened by the Early Childhood Unit at the National Children's Bureau (NCB) which is a specialist body that supports quality improvement through a series of regional networks which share resources and work through local concerns and challenges, identifying what works and disseminating this to other local authorities and organisations. The Young Children's Voices Network (YCVN), also at the NCB, was set up to develop, promote and share good practice in listening to young children with the aim of ensuring that all early childhood services embed a culture of listening. Like many networks they offer training, support and advice as well as useful resources and tools.

Another more local example is that of childminding networks in which each group is made up of registered childminders, supported by a network coordinator and which provides organised social and learning activities for childminders and children as well as information, advice and support. The London Early Years Music Network meets every term to unite all those with an interest in music-making with young children. Some local authorities provide a specific forum for early years special educational needs coordinators (SENCos) and equal opportunities coordinators within settings. In some areas, individual settings are used to provide models of practice and can become inclusion 'hubs' where local resources and expertise are held.

Case study N2

The Early Years Teaching Centres Consortium helped to set up an Early Years Improvement Group for Birmingham, and is now leading on the development of an Early Years Improvement Strategy for the city. The group includes a collaboration of the 26 nursery schools in the city, children's centre teachers, early years consultants, children's centre area managers, primary heads, and early years teacher centre representatives, and reports to the Children's Trust Board, allowing them a clear voice in determining how Birmingham takes early years quality improvement forward.

A key part of the strategy is the early years networks in each of the 16 localities across the city, led by nursery schools and children's centres. Monthly network meetings support professional development across a wide range of areas, including assessment and moderation, transition, parental engagement, creativity, etc. These bring together private voluntary and independent (PVI) settings, schools, childminding network coordinators, family support champions, and early years consultants to support teaching and learning across all early years settings in the locality.

Further support is provided through a 'team around the setting' approach within each locality, which may take the form of visits to settings, modelling good practice, or specific tailored training. This brings together school and service improvement teams, helping settings to receive the support that they need – in all types of setting, and therefore for all children.

If there is no network that meets your needs locally or nationally then it may be helpful to set up your own group. Training and conferences are often a useful opportunity to link with those who share specific aims and concerns.

References

Coulson, A. (1985) *The Fear of Change.* Unpublished paper.

Moyles, J. (2006) *Effective Leadership and Management in the Early Years.* Maidenhead: Open University Press.

Plant, R. (1987) *Managing Change and Making it Stick.* London: Fontana.

Rodd, J. (1994) *Leadership in Early Childhood.* Maidenhead: Open University Press.

Siraj-Blatchford, I. and Manni, L. (2007) *Effective Leadership in the Early Years Sector: The ELEYS Study.* London: Institute of Education.

O

Observation
Outreach

Observation

Observation is best defined as a way of seeing that is informed by experience and professional knowledge. In early years practice it is a systematic way of observing the external behaviour of children usually involving sustained viewing. We do this in order to become more aware of children's development, abilities and how they view reality. This process is crucial in helping us to understand how we might support and extend an individual child's development and learning.

Observation can contribute to our understanding of the personal, social and emotional needs of children by enabling us to record the different persona and ways of being they adopt in response to the different contexts and relationships in which they find themselves. It can thus enable us to give all children a voice, especially those who for some reason or another cannot verbally communicate their own needs effectively. Regular observations of individual children can enable staff to share and demonstrate the validity of the child's experience and learning. In addition to enabling us to monitor progress of children's all-round development, this process can help us to evaluate our own provision and practice and help to determine staff development needs.

As Fawcett (Fawcett 2009: 9) points out, observation of children and the recording of their behaviour has a long and notable tradition that includes luminaries such as Rousseau, Pestalozzi, Darwin and Freud, right through to more modern theorists such as Piaget, Bruner and Vygotsky. In terms of inclusive practice, how we observe and why and the conclusions that we draw can be crucial to the progress and development of individual children, especially as the process of observation is so often linked to some form of assessment.

Observation continues to be a key tool in research of all kinds and, as Roberts-Holmes (2005) argues, that observation enables the researcher to see familiar or routine events in different ways. He argues:

> In a similar way critical looking and listening in research demands that you try to make familiar everyday behaviour that seems 'normal', distant and strange. By making everyday events unfamiliar and foreign to you, you will be engaging in critical observation. Through your readings and your observations you should try to open up and see everyday situations that you take as normal in a different light.
>
> (Roberts-Holmes, 2005: 93–94)

In order to be a successful observer of children it is important to be aware of the subjective nature of how we are receiving and interpreting the information we are gathering. Fawcett (2009: 21) writes about the importance of reflecting on our own attitudes and the assumptions we might be making as a consequence:

> First then, we must recognise that we all have different ethnic or national origin, age, class, religion, physical appearance, gender and sexual orientation. Second we need to consider where we are in relation to others; where we stand in society; the personal power we have, and how we perceive others from different groups. Finally, we must inform ourselves about the structural oppressions in society.

Drummond (1993) cites the work of Margaret Lowenfeld, an early childhood expert who was highly influential in the 1930s. She identified four ways in which the human mind can make errors in observation (Drummond 1993: 71, citing Lowenfeld 1935):

- The mind cannot grasp that which is wholly unfamiliar to it.
- The mind is more apt to see that which it has already noticed.
- The mind is unable to see that which it has not been trained to accept.
- The mind unconsciously distorts what it hears and sees, according to its own prejudices.

In saying this Lowenfeld also reminds us of the importance of self-knowledge and an open mind in relation to what we observe. For most practitioners observation is a feature of their everyday working life. All sorts of ad hoc observations may contribute to practice in an informal way but specific observations, especially those which are intended to clarify a child's current level of performance and skills mastered, will probably need to be planned.

Different authors, different researchers and different fields of work all use a different form of words to describe the ways and means by which evidence can be accumulated. However, in early years practice it is likely to include the following:

- Participant observation – where the observer is involved in activities with the children.
- 'Catch as you can' type observations, taking place 'on the hop' and/or when the practitioner is not directly involved with the child.
- Notes on significant achievement.
- Longer observations, for example, if there has been a specific concern expressed about the child.
- Observations from parents.
- Conversations with children.

Practice example O1

Archie came to Leadbury nursery when he was two and a half. His behaviour immediately gave grounds for concern both in the setting and, as his mother reported, at home. His key worker made a number of narrative and ad hoc observations during routine activities which revealed that Archie enjoyed problem solving especially puzzles and loves to look at pictures in books.

However, some aspects of his behaviour were obsessive; he had difficulty with following set routine and became anxious when introduced to new situations and people. The information gained was used to contribute to an individual educational plan (IEP) in which social and emotional issues were a specific priority and targeted strategies were adopted by all staff to ensure a consistent response to his behavioural issues.

As time passed Archie was observed to be exhibiting a delay in speech development and this was contributing significantly to the frustration and upset he often expressed. In conjunction with the parents, staff instigated a Common Assessment Framework (CAF) which led to support through the local speech and language therapy service and from an educational psychologist, and the family was also referred to a specialist outreach service aimed at families in their situation.

From the work undertaken by the nursery and these agencies a diagnosis for autistic spectrum disorder was made and appropriate support was put in place including a 25-hour statement which allowed him to have the one to one assistance needed at times for him to progress.

Observation has been highlighted earlier in this book as an important strand of the process of listening to young children with all the benefits this entails. Play based assessment (PBA) can be useful because it enables us to observe children in more natural situations and is more likely to give us sensitive insights than a more formal test situation or an environment in which the child is unfamiliar. Sayeed and Guerin (2000: 49) see PBA as an approach that combines observation and adult participation which is accessible to parents and professionals in a range of contexts. The PBA enables adults to conduct assessments through the child's familiar play situation. However, PBA has been criticised in the past because observations may be highly subjective and now various checklists have been produced to overcome this problem.

There is a vast array of observational methods but two worthy of note in this context are the Leuven approach and the High/Scope Anecdotal record. The Leuven approach was developed by Ferre Laevers who sought to monitor children's involvement in learning as a key indicator of well-being. Using this approach the practitioner needs to be aware of a range of specific 'involvement' signals. Laevers (1994: 61) describes the concept of 'Involvement' as 'a quality of human activity, characterised by concentration and persistence, a high level of motivation, intense perceptions and experiences of meanings, a strong flow of energy, a high degree of satisfaction, and based on the exploratory drive and basic development of schemes'.

High/Scope is a long established educational approach that is used in over 20 countries. The approach centres on the recognition and support of unique differences in children and aims to support the development of self-esteem and confidence. The High/Scope Anecdotal record entails daily records for individual children who are observed for 10 to 15 minutes each day. These records are used within the team in order to reflect on what has been seen and heard that day, and this builds to a summative record over time. Assessment is then recorded against defined key learning experiences and takes the form of an observational checklist which details the developmental steps involved in progressing through each key learning experience

Any information we gather from observation can be used for monitoring, evaluation and future planning. Effective observation allows us to create optimum environments for each child based on individual need and to take appropriate action if there is any reason for concern. It is also essential, in some form, when reviewing the curriculum and projected outcomes for individual children

Outreach

The term 'hard to reach' is often used by local authorities and organisations to describe groups who are more likely to be socially excluded, including homeless people, Travellers, asylum seekers, refugees, disabled people, prisoners, people with mental health issues or indeed anyone who is perceived as living within the margins of society. Sometimes fathers come into this category as they are often harder to engage by conventional means.

Many who support these minority groups and the members of these groups themselves find this term a misnomer as the reality is that it is the services themselves that are hard to access. Without a doubt there are still gaps in our understanding of what persuades and motivates families to access certain provision and often those most in need of services, including those who lack informal support, are the least likely to access them (Ghate and Hazel 2002). The reasons for this situation are often complex and difficult to unravel. Research into outreach services done as part of the Sure Start evaluation (Ball and Niven 2006: 1) found that providers interpreted outreach services in four distinct ways:

- to inform families about what was available to help them
- to make services easier to reach and use
- to provide a gateway to persuade parents to access services
- to deliver services through home visits.

This study highlighted the importance of outreach services as a tool to engage marginalised families and found that outreach was generally more successful than other methods especially when trust was established with families who perceived the strategy as less 'stigmatising' and less 'interfering'.

Practice example 02

A family was referred to outreach support by a senior worker from a children's centre because the youngest child was prone to poor behaviour and aggressive outbursts. At first glance, these tantrums seemed to be the result of inconsistent parenting and that this was confusing the youngest child. Outreach support revealed a conflict between the mother and father, which made any form of consistent parenting difficult. In addition to the difficulties between the parents and the upbringing of the youngest child, the elder son was involved with a gang and stealing from the family.

In order to help the family resolve their issues, the family participated in weekly home visits from the family outreach worker. These visits provided an opportunity for the mother to discuss her feelings of isolation, her concerns relating to her oldest son, the difficulties faced in relation to her youngest daughter and the impact this was all having on family life. She was encouraged to be consistent in her parenting approaches to the young daughter, and the outreach worker helped her come up with strategies to support improvements in the child's behaviour. The mother also got help finding helpful resources for the eldest son.

The persistence of particular individuals such as community workers, interpreters, teachers and others was thought to be a key factor that could contribute to the successful engagement with hitherto marginalised families. There was also the necessary task of enthusing families about their own children's potential and helping the adults to see beyond their own difficulties. Although many settings do not have the resources or person power for systematic outreach, it remains a potentially powerful tool for services that are determined to be representative of their communities and to engage successfully all relevant groups.

References

Ball, M. and Niven, L. (2006) *National Evaluation Report: Outreach and Home-Visiting Services in Sure Start Local Programmes.* London: Department for Education and Skills.

Drummond, M.J. (1993) *Assessing Children's Learning.* London: David Fulton.

Fawcett, M. (2009) *Learning Through Child Observation,* 2nd edn. London: Jessica Kingsley Publishers.

Ghate, D. and Hazel, N. (2002) *Parenting in Poor Environments: Stress, Support and Coping.* London: Jessica Kingsley Publishers.

Laevers, F. (ed.) (1994) *The Leuven Involvement Scale for Young Children.* Leuven: Centre for Experiential Education.

Lowenfeld, M . (1935) *Play in Childhood.* New York: Wiley.

Roberts-Holmes, G. (2005) *Doing Your Early Years Research Project. A Step-by-step Guide.* London: Sage.

Sayeed, Z. and Guerin, E. (2000) *Early Years Play.* London: David Fulton.

P

Parental involvement
Parenting and disability
Poverty

Parental involvement

The term parent is used here to denote anyone who is taking on the parenting role of a child. Research in the *Effective Provision of Pre-schools Education* (Sylvia et al. 2004) has shown the positive impact of parental involvement on children's learning and achievement. The evidence indicates that parental involvement benefits not only children themselves but also the teachers/practitioners, the setting and the parents themselves.

In a review of the research Desforges and Abuchaar (2003) showed that young children whose parents are involved in their learning have better language skills and are more numerate than those whose parents are not. Some of the key findings are summarised below:

- In the early years, parents' involvement has a significant impact on children's cognitive development, literacy and number skills.
- Parent involvement in a child's schooling for a child between 7 and 16 is a more powerful force than family background, size of family and the level of parental education.
- Parental involvement has a significant effect on pupil achievement throughout the school years.
- The extent and form of parental involvement is influenced by family social class, maternal level of education, material deprivation, maternal health and status (e.g. single parent) and to a lesser degree by family ethnicity.
- Educational failure is increased by lack of parental interest in schooling.
- Most parents believe that the responsibility for their child's education is shared between parents and the school.
- Many parents want to be involved in their children's education.

Although there is no universal agreement about what constitutes parental involvement, it usually includes not only being interested in the life and activities of the setting but also by supporting the child in conjunction with the setting. The term 'partnership' is often used in relation to how settings should work with parents and has been enshrined in legislation and guidance. Current thinking about partnership with parents is that parents should be viewed as experts on their child and that their knowledge and experience should be equivalent and complementary to those who have other expertise to offer.

For writers such as Wolfendale, despite the fact that those who work with parents of disabled children are constantly exhorted to be 'partners', the concept is at best a slippery one. Wolfendale (1989: 107–117) describes the elements or building blocks of partnership (as perceived by various writers) to be as follows:

- equality in decision making
- power sharing
- equal rights in self-expression
- the exercise of mutual responsibility and accountability by all parties.

The evidence is that these preconditions are rarely evident in the early experiences of most families. As Wolfendale later observes, these elements are extremely difficult to graft on to any exclusive, hierarchical bureaucratic system.

An Audit Commission study (2003) also found that parents of disabled children noticed a tendency for professionals to talk to each other with language that parents could not understand. Parents often felt that their own expertise in caring for their child and knowing his or her needs was being overlooked in favour of fixed professional views and procedures.

In 2001 the National Family and Parenting Institute found that some specific groups were less likely to access services than others (Hendricson et al. 2001). These were fathers, disabled parents, parents of teenagers, Black and minority ethnic (BME) families, asylum-seeking parents, homeless or peripatetic families and rural families. Research by the Rowntree Foundation (Katz et al. 2007: 7) categorised the barriers to inclusion for these groups as follows:

- Physical and practical barriers – not being aware of services or physically being unable to access the service due to transport difficulties or physical barriers to accessing premises such as stairs.
- Social barriers – these include language, cultural and institutional barriers such as attitudes and poverty.

Suspicion and stigma with regard to services is also an important barrier, especially for parenting programmes which parents fear may lead to them being labelled as failed parents for participating. A recent study (Hunt et al. 2011) found that significant barriers to engaging parents were identified by staff, including parents lacking time, having had negative experiences of an educational environment, parents lacking confidence and/or having English as an additional language.

Practice example P1

Danny is four and has persistently been getting into disagreements and confrontations with staff and other children. His parents have little involvement with the nursery and he is usually brought and collected by his older sister. Staff make a video of examples of Danny's positive and negative behaviour and invite his parents in to see the result.

In discussion with his parents, staff find that Danny has been encouraged to 'stick up for himself' and to use aggression in order to get what he wants at home. He comes from a large family in which it is difficult to make his voice heard and he is often involved in play fighting with his brothers in which the boundaries are not always clear.

Staff work with his parents in order to make clear the nursery ethos and policy on behaviour. They encourage Danny to articulate his needs without aggression and to learn to share and take turns with other children. His parents are encouraged to take part in nursery activities and events, to ask questions about strategies and communicate with staff more effectively. These approaches combine to produce a dramatic improvement in Danny's behaviour, both at home and in the setting.

Whalley (2001) discusses the various methods of recording involvement of parents and carers at the Pen Green centre. By monitoring those parents who are involved, this has helped to identify non-attendees such as fathers/male carers. This approach also enabled the staff to determine which services were proving more popular. Whalley (2001: 53) was able to identify within her centre those parents who did not get involved. It was found that the factors that may have impinged on their involvement and participation could be any one or combination of the following:

- Marital status.
- The parent's employment patterns.
- Language barriers.
- Family pressure.
- Whether the child has one or two years in the nursery.
- Whether the parent/carer had a previous child in the nursery.
- Parents' apparent hostility to any interventions.
- Parents' education experience.
- The family worker's personality.
- Changes in family life.

Although parents should be recognised as the first educators of their children and hold considerable expertise and knowledge in relation to them, they may also hold opinions, beliefs and values that are contrary to the values of the setting and at times these may even seem to be at odds with the rights of their children, as perceived by staff. For example, some parents are not in favour of a play-based curriculum, preferring a more formal, structured approach. The management of children's behaviour within the setting could also become an issue for parents as it may differ from their own value system. The question arises here as to whether parents are *always* the best advocates for their children. Some examples of where opinions could differ with parents and practitioners are as follows:

- A Jehovah's Witness family has given strict instructions for their child not to partake in the celebrations of birthdays and Christmas.
- A parent has requested that her child can be reprimanded with a smack if he or she misbehaves.
- A parent has requested that a child says his or her prayers before meals.
- A parent insists on bringing a hot, home cooked meal into the school at lunchtime, rather than giving his or her child a lunchbox of cold food or paying for a school dinner.

When developing inclusive practice it is useful to try to anticipate such scenarios so that clear and understandable policy objectives are set and shared with families and staff from the outset.

Parenting and disability

It is important to remember that parents of disabled children are individuals and will therefore experience the disability of their child in individual ways. However, from the experiences that many parents describe it is possible to discern certain patterns. Children who are born with a disability are not usually welcomed into the world with the same joy and acceptance as other children. As Dickins (2013) points out, they are often greeted as 'bad news' by relatives and the general public. In addition they may be treated as a 'tragedy' or seen as problematic by the medical profession who often see their primary role as 'making good' such deficits and impairments rather than also supporting the emotional adjustment of parents. Many parents still struggle to overcome the effects of negative interpretations of disability which are all too often reinforced by the attitudes and assumptions of those around them (Wall 2003).

There is a huge variation across the UK in terms of the services available to support families. While some families have experienced positive professional intervention, others have found it inadequate, invasive or inappropriate or that key services are not available at all. Encountering professionals who have a positive attitude and are willing to understand, listen and build trust can be an important step forward for families.

For some children their impairments will be apparent from birth or before; for others the impairments will develop or become apparent gradually. Some children and families will have high expectations for future development, especially if appropriate support is available, but for others the prognosis may be one of increasing difficulty and reduced life expectancy. Increasingly the term 'global delay' is used where there is no clear diagnosis of impairment and/or condition. It is probably true to say that for many children their future development cannot be reliably predicted and this unavoidable uncertainty can be the cause of considerable family distress.

Being the parent of a disabled child is not an easy task in today's society. Evidence from the campaigning charity Contact a Family (Bennet 2009: 5) found that negative attitudes towards disability coupled with a lack of services were the main barriers which impacted on the quality of life for families. Amongst the key findings are the following:

- Almost 70 per cent of respondents said that understanding and acceptance of disability from their community or society is poor or unsatisfactory.
- Over 60 per cent of families said they don't feel listened to by professionals.
- Over 60 per cent of families said they don't feel valued by society in their role as carers.
- Half of families with disabled children said the opportunity to enjoy play and leisure together is poor or unsatisfactory.

In addition, when Contact a Family (2012: 3) asked over 2000 UK families caring for a disabled child about their current financial situation they found the following results:

- One in six families (17 per cent) are going without food.
- More than one in five families (21 per cent) are going without heating.
- A quarter (26 per cent) are going without specialist equipment or adaptations.
- 86 per cent have gone without leisure and days out.
- One in five families had been threatened with court action because of non-payment of bills, including essential such as utilities.

More recently, Dickins (2013) draws attention to the potentially negative impact for many families of UK benefit changes such as the introduction of Universal Credit. Research by Chamba et al. (1999) found that overall families caring for a severely disabled child from minority ethnic groups were even more disadvantaged than White families in similar situations, although families' experiences varied across ethnic groups.

It is natural for any parent to be saddened by loss of expectations for their children. It is hard to be positive when faced with immediate difficulties of practical care and a sense of isolation and rejection. Currently we are seeing an increase in the rate of survival of children with complex needs whose physical care requires stamina and constant attention. It is amazing that so many parents come through and cope so well.

Micheline Mason (2008: 27) writes powerfully from her perspective as a disabled parent and the parent of a disabled child about the barriers created by the medical model of disability through which disabled children are regarded as problematic and faulty: 'Underlying the "medical model" are the values of the most powerful classes of people, i.e. that our worth as human beings is only in our capacity to be economically productive'. This view is supported by many commentators including Runswick-Cole (2008: 176) who explains:

> A medical model framework emerges from models used in medicine in which practitioners think in terms of 'conditions', 'treatment', 'cure' and 'rehabilitation'. A medical model assumes that the disabled adult or child is deficient but, it is hoped, alterable; whereas society is fixed, with limited capacity for, or willingness to change.

In contrast Mason (2008) describes the social model as less concerned with the disabling effects of impairments and more concerned with the barriers to ordinary life that can be removed through collective social action.

Susan le Poidevin (Le Poivedin and Cameron 1985: 190–201), who herself lost her sight in adulthood, developed a model of 'disability adjustment counselling'. She applies this to parents and disabled adults and lists the following areas of adjustment:

- Intellectual: acceptance of the fact and implications of disability.
- Psychological: formation of a satisfactory identity and self-concept.
- Spiritual: redefinition of philosophy, purpose and meaning of life, making sense of loss, faith.
- Emotional: development of child's emotional stability and security, restoration of emotional balance.
- Behavioural: reorganisation of routine and lifestyle with minimum disruption.
- Social: reorganisation of family structure, adaptation to changes of role and status.
- Practical: adaptation to the practical demands of daily living.

Whilst the onus of adjustment here is on the individual family or person, the social model of disability encourages us all to adapt and to see disability and many of its consequences as socially constructed. Whilst this may help us a great deal to develop more sensitive, enabling and effective services for families, it does not make the grief and sense of loss for the 'expected' child any less real or painful for those parents who experience it.

Case study P2

Parents for Inclusion is a network of parents of disabled children and children categorised as having 'special' needs. As an organisation they have worked together with disabled people with the aim of building inclusive communities in ordinary life, where all people are truly welcome. They provide a helpline, training, inclusion groups in schools and parent representation and maintain strong links with the inclusion movement.

Parents for Inclusion engages with parents and professionals in a way which places the child's views and wishes at the centre of action; fully supports, and promotes the social model of disability; works together with disabled people as equals – as partners, colleagues, in relationships and friendships and creates allies amongst disabled people, parents and professionals

(Adapted from Parents for Inclusion 2013)

It has been estimated that there are 1.1 million households with dependant children that have at least one disabled parent (Social Care Institute for Excellence 2006). The absence of reliable statistics is amongst the factors that have caused the needs of this important minority to be generally neglected. Their job as parents is generally unsupported by mainstream services, especially childcare provision, or by the education system which may be accessible to their children but excludes them.

For example a study undertaken by the Task Force on Supporting Disabled Adults in their Parenting Role (Morris 2003) received evidence that people with learning difficulties, physical and sensory impairment, mental health difficulties, long-term illness, HIV/AIDS experienced long-term barriers to receiving appropriate support in their parenting role. The study took evidence from parents, professional and researchers and this is what was revealed:

- Policies and services concerning adults and/or children are commonly developed without consulting or involving disabled parents.
- Disabled parents find it difficult to access information and advice, advocacy and peer support.
- There are particular problems with the relationship between children's services and adults' community care services. Work is required at both national and local level to create the framework for more appropriate service responses.
- Disabled adults sometimes find it difficult to access their entitlements to support under community care legislation. This can lead to them having to rely on their children for assistance (i.e. their children become 'young carers').

- Although assistance with parenting tasks should be available within the current community care framework, disabled people are often told that they can only access support through children and families services.
- Parents often find they can only get a response from services when things reach a crisis, at which point they can be at risk of losing their children into care.
- Mental health policy and practice does not adequately address the fact that many people with mental health support needs are parents.
- Direct payments can provide the flexible support needed but much work remains to be done to increase the numbers of parents receiving direct payments, particularly those from minority ethnic communities, those with learning difficulties and those with mental health support needs.
- Disabled parents experience unequal access to health (including maternity care) and other mainstream services for parents and their children.
- Disability benefits do not take account of the additional costs of parenting for disabled adults.

(McGaw 2004: 215)

The lack of awareness in both the planning and delivery of services can further disadvantage these parents who are already struggling within a hostile system. Olsen and Clarke's (2003) study argues that planners should recognise the importance of family context and not simply focus on individual needs. They plead for innovative policies that direct services to take a 'life-course perspective', addressing the changing demands of the parenting role and supporting family relationships.

One example is that all prospective parents are encouraged to find out about local schools by visiting them. However, as Jenny Morris (2003: 8) observes, many disabled parents experience significant difficulties when they try to do this. Sometimes these difficulties are a result of unhelpful attitudes. When one parent who uses a wheelchair turned up at an open day for a tour of a school, she was informed by the head teacher: 'Two sets of wheels – that's a problem. I do a fast tour, you'll never keep up'. Another parent who has difficulty walking said: 'On the first-year tours, I'm always left behind in the hall, not looking at the school facilities with other parents'.

Practice example P3

When Harry and his mother, who is physically disabled and uses a wheelchair, visit Gateway Nursery staff do their best to make the entrance, which has a small step, accessible through the provision of a temporary ramp so that she can come through the front door like other parents. Harry's mother also has a hearing impairment but can lip-read fluently so staff make sure that they are positioned correctly when speaking to her and check for subsequent understanding. They are keen to identify other adjustments and modifications which might be helpful should Harry subsequently attend the setting.

Providers need to understand that physical access is not only about level or ramped access for parents with mobility impairments. It is also about lighting and colour contrasts which make it easier for visually impaired people to enter and move around a building, and hearing loops especially for meetings and events. Other difficulties that disabled parents may face include inaccessible forms and procedures, doorbells and switches they cannot reach and negative attitudes about their ability to communicate or parent effectively. Parents with learning disabilities, for example, are often considered incapable of parenting and can be at risk of having their parental responsibilities terminated on the basis of evidence that would not be used against non-disabled parents. Family and childcare problems are sometimes ascribed to the limitations of the parents rather than environmental pressures or shortcomings in the support systems.

Poverty

The concepts of 'absolute' and 'relative' poverty are crucial to our current understanding of what poverty is all about. In Victorian times an influential attempt to define and respond to poverty was conducted by Booth and Rowntree, who were both well-known philanthropists of that era. Their work focused on the concept of absolute poverty where the ability to maintain good health was constrained by the lack of income. The term 'absolute' poverty is understood as a basic level of poverty where there is a struggle to meet minimum standards of food, clothing, health care and shelter necessary to maintain life. By contrast 'relative' poverty refers to a standard which is defined in terms of the individual society and this may differ and change between countries and over a period of time. In simplistic terms the concept of absolute poverty is that there are minimum standards below which no one anywhere in the world should ever fall. The concept of relative poverty is that, in a relatively rich country such as the UK, there are higher minimum standards below which no one should fall, and that these standards should rise if the country becomes richer.

According to the Child Poverty Action Group there are 3.6 million children in the UK living in poverty today and in certain places between 50 and 70 per cent of children are growing up in poverty. (CPAG 2012). People become poor for many reasons and although the media portrayal is often one of drug and alcohol dependency, family breakdown and a culture of worklessness and benefit dependency, the true picture is far more complex. Current strategies for welfare reform have been criticised as being founded on the moralistic Victorian notion of the 'undeserving' poor which begs the important question as to whether children should suffer for their parents' behaviour, however much society disapproves of their lifestyle and choices.

It is also important to recognise that there is a rise in those working families who are being affected by poverty and also the increasing cost of childcare. In 2011 Save the Children and Daycare Trust surveyed 4000 families and found that

80 per cent of parents surveyed agreed with the statement 'Once I have paid for childcare, I am in a similar position to as if I was not working', and a quarter of parents said that, regardless of incomes, the cost of childcare has caused them to get into debt (Save the Children/Daycare Trust 2011). Poverty is an experience that anyone from any social background or class can undergo. However, class itself is often an indicator of life chances and future wealth. Poverty can lead to deprivation and social exclusion where individuals are excluded from the benefits of mainstream society.

There is no doubt that poverty can blight childhoods and have serious convoluted consequences in the longer term. The Child Poverty Action Group (2012: 1) observes that amongst the effects are the following:

- By the age of three , poorer children are estimated to be, on average, nine months behind children from more wealthy backgrounds.
- By 16, children receiving free schools meals achieve 1.7 grades lower at GCSE.
- Children living in poverty are almost twice as likely to live in bad housing. This has significant effects on both their physical and mental health, as well as educational achievement (Rice 2006).
- The health consequences of poverty can also be severe.

An improvement in the material circumstances of UK children in poverty looks unlikely at present. Maggie Atkinson, the Children's Commissioner for England (Office of the Children's Commissioner 2012) raises concerns with regard to the benefits cap and argues that it constitutes a contravention of Article 26 of the United Nations Convention on the Rights of the Child which guarantees the right to social security. The paper predicts a possible increase in child poverty with associated poor health, education and other outcomes; children losing their home as a result of unaffordability; the breakdown of families and communities and a disproportionate impact on children from some Black minority ethnic groups; disabled children and children of disabled parents and children living with kinship carers.

Whilst it is generally recognised that child poverty is increasing, the ways in which we assess, understand and address poverty are increasingly the subject of conflicting debate and analysis. A consensus is developing, however, that the immediate future will be difficult not only for families traditionally thought of as 'deprived' but also for those 'working poor' whose income is becoming increasingly stretched through price rises and pay cuts or freezes.

Individual settings are limited in the steps that they can take to offset the consequences of poverty in the local area but the provision of clothes swaps, breakfast clubs and a sympathetic environment in which parents can talk through their concerns and anxieties can help a great deal from day to day. A concerted local authority approach such as the example below can offset some of the difficulties and make a big difference to families.

Case study P4

The London Borough of Islington has one of the highest rates of child poverty in the UK with approximately 46 per cent of children living in poverty. Islington Council has made child poverty a high priority, with each service making an explicit commitment to play a role in reducing child poverty and mitigating its effects. The following key elements are the main focus:

- Early intervention through children's centres – engaging parents of children under four in pre-employment activities.
- Better use of local data and intelligence to target interventions.
- Improved effectiveness and efficiency through better partnership working and alignment of budgets.
- Embedding child poverty and parental employment objectives in mainstream services so that action on child poverty is sustainable.
- Ensuring strong corporate leadership.

The following strategies are proving to be effective, especially in improving take up of services:

- Delivering targeted pre-employment services for parents through children's centres has seen a significant increase in take-up of the children's centre core offer by disadvantaged families. A survey of parents has shown a high level of satisfaction with employment support delivered through the children's centres.
- There is continued engagement and training for both council staff and partners on child poverty and a range of people have been trained, including a GP, drugs and alcohol workers, joint visiting team officers and others for Islington staff.

The aspiration is to continue to link back to managers and staff who have been on the training and review what changes they have made to ensure that the needs of parents are always identified so they can receive the right signposting to move them closer to the labour market.

Source: adapted from Department for Education (2012)

References

Audit Commission (2003) *Services for Disabled Children.* London: Audit Commission.
Bennet, E. (2009) *What Makes My Family Stronger.* London: Contact a Family.
Chamba, R., Ahmad, W., Hirst, M., Lawton, L. and Beresford, B. (1999) *On the Edge: Minority Ethnic Families Caring for a Severely Disabled Child.* London: Policy Press.
Child Poverty Action Group (CPAG, 2012) *The Impact of Poverty.* www.cpag.org.uk/content/impact-poverty (accessed 1 February 2013).

Contact a Family (2012) *Counting the Costs 2012 – The Financial Reality for Families with Disabled Children across the UK.* www.cafamily.org.uk/media/381221/counting_the _costs_2012_full_report.pdf (accessed 3 February 2013).

Department for Education (DfE, 2012) *Integrating Services to Tackle Child Poverty.* www. education.gov.uk/childrenandyoungpeople/families/childpoverty/sharinggoodpractice/ a0069246/integrating-services-to-tackle-child-poverty (accessed 1 February 2013).

Desforges, C. and Abuchaar, A. (2003) *The Impact of Parental Involvement, Parental Support and Family Education on Pupil Achievement and Adjustment.* London: Department for Education and Skill.

Dickins, M. (2013) Supporting the well-being of children with disabilities and their families, in J. Manning-Morton (ed.) *Exploring Well-being in the Early Years.* Maidenhead: Open University Press.

Henricson, C., Katz, I., Mesie, J., Sandison, M. and Tunstill, J. (2001) *National Mapping of Services in England and Wales: A Consultation Document.* London: NFPI.

Hunt, S., Virgo, S., Klett-Davies, M., Page, A. and Apps, J. (2011) *Provider Influence on the Early Home Learning Environment.* London: Family and Parenting Institute.

Katz, I., La Placa, V. and Hunter, S. (2007) *Barriers to Inclusion and Successful Engagement of Parents in Mainstream Services.* London: Policy Research Bureau.

Le Poivedin, S. and Cameron, J. (1985) Is there more to portage than education?, in F. Daly (eds) *Portage: The Importance of Parents.* Windsor: NFER Nelson.

Mason, M. (2008) *Dear Parents.* Nottingham: Inclusive Solutions.

Morris, J. (2003) *Supporting Disabled Adults in their Parenting Role.* York: Joseph Rowntree Foundation.

McGraw, S. (2004) Parenting exceptional children, in Hoghughi, M. and Long, N. (eds) *Handbook of Parenting: Theory and Research for Practice.* London: Sage.

Office of the Children's Commissioner (OCC, 2012) *A Child Rights Impact Assessment of the Welfare Reform Bill.* London: Office of Children's Commissioner.

Olsen, R. and Clarke, H. (2003) *Parenting and Disability: Disabled Parents' Experiences of raising Children.* Bristol: The Policy Press.

Parents for Inclusion www.parentsforinclusion.org/aboutPi.htm (accessed 14 May 2013).

Rice, B. (2006) *Against the Odds.* London: Shelter.

Runswick-Cole, K. (2008) Between a rock and a hard place: parents' attitudes to the inclusion of children with special educational needs in mainstream and special schools, *British Journal of Special Education,* 35(3): 173–180.

Save the Children/ Daycare Trust (2011) *Making Work pay – The Children Trap.* London: Save the Children.

Sylva, K., Melhuish, E., Sammons, P., Siraj-Blatchford, I. and Taggart, B. (2004) *Effective Provision of Pre-school Education (EPPE) Project: Final Report.* London: DfES.

Social Care Institute for Excellence (2006) *Supporting Disabled Parents and Parents with Additional Support Needs.* London: Social Care Institute for Excellence.

Wall, K. (2003) *Special Needs and Early Years.* London: Paul Chapman.

Whalley, M. (2001) *Involving Parents in their Children's Learning.* London: Sage.

Wolfendale, S. (1989) Parental involvement and power-sharing in special needs, in S. Wolfendale *Parental Involvement - Developing Networks between Home, School and Community.* London: Cassell.

Quality in early education
Questions that children ask

Quality in early education

There are numerous studies (Osborn and Milbank 1987; Sylva et al. 2004, 2010) that suggest that quality of provision is linked to better outcomes for young children in terms of both social adjustment and later achievement. Participation in high-quality education has been demonstrated to reduce the negative effects of poverty and disadvantage (Sylva et al. 2004). However, a key international debate in early childhood is focused on the ways in which we determine what constitutes quality provision and indeed whose idea of quality it is that we should be pursuing.

If we view the education and care of young children as a passive process of preparation for school then we are likely to focus on measurable and quantifiable learning outcomes as a primary means of determining quality. On the other hand, if we take a more holistic view of the child we may want to prioritise social and emotional development and the overall well-being of children as a determinant of quality pre-school provision. So how we view quality is to a great extent dependent on how we view childhood itself and what we consider that the priorities for early childhood provision should be. Arguably our current UK system relies on subjective measures and has a clear focus on children as an investment in the future and childcare provision as a means of enabling parents to work. These priorities are hugely influential in determining what is regarded as quality of provision.

Dahlberg et al. (1999) have challenged the notion that quality can be universally defined and question whether it can be objectively evaluated. They identified two broad ways of thinking about quality. The first is the 'discourse of quality' (Dahlberg et al. 1999: 87) which regards quality as associated with specific outcomes and the structures that can enable those outcomes to be met. This is evident in current education policy and thinking with prescribed outcomes in curriculum document that set targets and developmental goals from birth.

The second is the 'discourse of meaning making' which is more concerned with gaining a deeper understanding of childhood, how it is that practitioners work with children and what we can learn from this. According to this view, positive and secure relationships are central and the way in which we determine quality should involve a dynamic and ongoing process of discussion and debate. This debate, in turn, should reflect the experiences and wishes of the children, their carers and those who work with them, rather than being driven by an unquestioning acceptance of traditional givens and 'truths' about childhood itself.

Hines (2008: 166) explains how a focus on economic and social targets is at odds with the idea of a 'discourse of meaning making' because the outcomes would not be measurable or quantifiable. She observes:

> The measurable outcomes that exist are not always meaningful to the lives of children and their carers. The vision of quality that is embedded in Ofsted frameworks and the outcomes for children may not be shared by all families because of the variety of social and cultural backgrounds. This vision of quality may not improve access for these groups unless they are part of the discussion of what provision should be like.

The influential Effective Provision of Pre-school Education Project (EPPE)(Sylva et al. 2004) found that good-quality pre-school education can be found in all kinds of settings irrespective of the type provided, although children tended to make better intellectual progress in fully integrated nurseries and schools. The quality of the interactions between children and staff were particularly important. The researchers used direct observations combined with formal analysis of structural dimensions in order to determine elements of quality, thus incorporating both qualitative and quantitative methodologies. They used 'value added' methods which took account of factors such as home learning environment, parental qualifications and occupations, home language and gender in order to make appropriate comparisons across a range of settings. They found that having qualified teachers who took the role as pedagogical leaders to have had the biggest impact on quality.

Alexander (2010) demonstrates just how variable practitioners' perceptions of quality are by using the concept of the 'successful child' to explore the practitioners 'sense' of the children they worked with and the aspirations they held for them. Whilst all the participants of the study regarded a 'happy' child as a successful child, they varied considerably in what they meant by this. For example, in one setting, a Foundation Stage Unit in a school, a 'happy' and therefore successful child was characterised as one who did not attract negative attention from adults. In other settings such as children's centres, a child was regarded as happy and successful if they could communicate effectively and form positive relationships and select and develop activities in a satisfying way. Alexander (2010: 113) goes on to compare these perceptions to the school perspective:

> The successful school child has relationships with adults that are positive, often framed within the discourse of school that construes children as pupils who follow the rules and know precisely where the boundaries of acceptable behaviour are.

Issues of classroom management enter the picture here with an emphasis put on independent and autonomous learners and those who were compliant. Overall it was found that criteria for judging success were: 'bounded by the contexts in which the practitioners work and by the professional identities constructed within those contexts and cultures'. Alexander concludes that adopting the idea of quality as subjective could actually help us value children's successes in broader terms that are not so restricted by external standards and accountability, although these are still seen as important.

The complex issues raised by this debate on quality cannot be done justice to here but the implications for how we determine the success or failure of inclusive practice, or indeed whether we consider inclusive values and principles as a factor at all, are clear. A system that defines the success or failure of provision purely in terms of narrow culturally bound educational outcomes is much less likely to value and promote the educational, social and emotional benefits of the inclusive approach.

Questions that children ask

> There is an inner voice that pushes children on, but this force is greatly multiplied when they are convinced that facts and ideas are resources, just as their friends and the adults in their lives are precious resources. It is especially at this point that children expect – as they have from the beginning of their life adventure – the help and truthfulness of grownups.
>
> (Loris Malaguzzi, from the catalogue of the exhibit 'The Hundred Languages of Children')

Children in an inclusive environment may ask questions about difference that have the capacity to make adults apprehensive and uncomfortable about how they should reply. As Magaluzzi exhorts in the quote above, in trying to make sense of the world around them children deserve honest and truthful answers. As we have seen previously, children are aware of differences and may be openly curious about them. 'Difficult' questions may also give insights into misunderstandings and confusion that requires clarification. As Brown points out (1998: 21):

> Children absorb misconceptions from the discriminatory actions and stereotypical attitudes they see and hear, as well as from the way adults respond

to their observations and questions about differences in skin colour and physical features.

Most young children will be curious, notice disabilities and other perceived differences and ask questions about them. Children need brief, honest, accurate answers. They may also need information, support and opportunities to discuss the issues and ask further questions. For example, children may be curious about the equipment and devices people use for specific disabilities and about what a child or adult with a particular impairment can or cannot do. Lane (2008: 94) stresses the importance of anticipating children's questions and gives the following examples:

> Why is Ahmed's skin dirty brown?
> Why does Selma's mummy have that black thing all over her? (Selma's mummy is Muslim and wears a chador).
> Why can't Adu speak English?

Lane (2008) stresses the importance of responding within a 'no-blame culture' and not making immediate assumptions about implied negativity. Questions about impairment can often provoke discomfort for adult carers, but most disabled children and adults are happy to talk to others about their impairments and differences. Working with Persona Dolls or using other projective techniques such as puppets can be a good way of raising issues of difference with children in order to stimulate questions. Although the time may not always be right, an honest answer is usually preferable to an embarrassed silence or swift changing of the subject, which is likely to give the child a negative message about issues that should be hidden or treated as taboo.

References

Alexander, E. (2010) A successful child: early years practitioners' understandings of quality, *Early Years*, 30(2): 107–118.

Brown, B. (1998) *Unlearning Discrimination in the Early Years*. Stoke-on-Trent: Trentham Books.

Dahlberg, G., Moss, P. and Pence, A. (1999) *Beyond Quality in Early Childhood Education and Care: Postmodern Perspectives*. London: Falmer Press.

Hines, C. (2008) Day care services for children, in P. Jones et al (eds) *Childhood: Services and Provision for Children*. Harlow: Pearson Education.

Lane, J. (2008) *Young Children and Racial Justice*. London: National Children's Bureau.

Osborn, A.F. and Milbank, J.E. (1987) *The Effects of Early Education*. Oxford: Oxford University Press.

Sylva, K., Melhuish, E., Sammons, P., Siraj Blatchford, I. and Taggart, B. (2004) *Effective Provision of Pre-school Education Project (EPPE): Final Report – A Longitudinal Study*. Nottingham: DfES Publications.

Sylva, K., Melhuish, E., Sammons, P., Siraj Blatchford, I. and Taggart, B. (2010) *Early Childhood Matters: Evidence from the Effective Pre-School and Primary Education Project*. London: Routledge.

R

Racism
Refugees and asylum seekers

Racism

Recognising that racism exists in society and that its effects on children and adults can be damaging and pervasive is an important step in creating an inclusive environment. The term racism is both difficult to define and often misused and misunderstood. Lane (2008: 31) offers us a useful working definition in the current context. She defines racism as: 'all those practices and procedures that, both historically and in the present, disadvantage and discriminate against people because of their skin colour, ethnicity, culture, religion, nationality or language'.

Most discussions of racism make the distinction between individual prejudice, bigotry and discrimination and that which is embedded in the institution and structures of society. Institutional or structural racism was recognised in the Macpherson Report into the case of Stephen Lawrence (Macpherson 1999) as the collective failure by an organisation to provide an effective and professional service to people just because of their culture, colour of skin or ethnic origin. A distinction also needs to be made here between racism against Black people and xenoracism, usually understood as hostility, prejudice and discrimination against people who are White. This issue will be discussed later on in this book.

In order to understand what racism is and what the implications are for young children and families we need also to understand the historical context in which negative ideas about Black people were formed. There is a long history of diversity in the UK, with the presence of Black and minority ethnic communities and individuals recorded from Roman times. Hostility and racism have also been demonstrated over the years. As far back as the sixteenth century Queen Elizabeth I complained about the number of 'blackamoors' in the country. In religious and popular culture blackness was always equated with evil. This reasoning was employed to justify the emerging slave trade and developed into 'scientific' theories of racial superiority as the UK took an increasing part in the slave trade during the eighteenth century.

In the twentieth century in Europe and the USA some practitioners of the newly emerging social sciences of psychology and sociology made fresh attempts to justify the concepts of racial superiority. Initially psychologists and sociologists attempted to explain complex social, political and economic processes in terms of the individual. More recently the focus for understanding both the development of prejudice and discrimination and ways to unlearn discrimination has been on cultural forces within a society, and how those forces influence the way in which the groups are perceived and valued.

After World War Two the need for reconstruction and the expansion of western European economies heralded a wave of migration to the UK in the 1950s. For many African Caribbean people migration seemed to offer the prospect of a better life. The reality they found was that Black people were expected to fill the jobs that the indigenous workforce was no longer willing to do in the servicing, semi-skilled and unskilled sectors. The blatant racism of employers and landlords contributed to a growing sense of alienation.

Recruitment campaigns also took place in India, Bangladesh and Pakistan. The immigrants arrived to find themselves perceived as 'dirty Pakis', 'coons' and 'wogs'. In an attempt to control such extreme responses the notion of assimilation was born: Black people were exhorted to become more like the indigenous White population. The argument was that if they became more acceptable, racism would be reduced.

Black children in school throughout the 1960s, 1970s and arguably to this day were subjected to stereotypical assumptions about their potential for achievement and behaviour. This is exemplified by the discovery in the late 1970s that a hugely disproportionate number of African Caribbean children were part of the segregated special school system – where access to the curriculum was profoundly limited and subsequent opportunities to enter the skilled labour force afterwards were limited or non-existent (Coard 1971).

In the late 1960s the influential Plowden Report concluded that while racial prejudice played little serious part in schools, it was clear that the needs of Black children were not being addressed. For many educators this was not simply a failure of assimilation but also reflected a value system in which certain children and their cultures were considered inferior. As a result many people working with children set up mechanisms to support them by sharing cultures, such as learning to cook a variety of foods, using clothes from many cultures in the dressing up corner and generally being more welcoming and friendly to one another. This was known as the 'multicultural' approach which had a big impact on early years provision and practice.

As early as 1989 Louise Derman-Sparkes argued that not only do young children notice and classify differences but they also begin to ascribe different values to groups of people according to the responses and behaviour of the adults and children around them. In *Children and Race: Ten Years On*, David Milner (1983) summarises the main theories of racial awareness and identity from the 1920s. Underpinning the most commonly accepted approaches to the development of racial identity in children is the work of Mary Ellen Goodman and Phylis Katz in the 1960s and 1970s (Goodman 1964; Katz 1973). Goodman proposed three stages of the acquisition of full racial awareness: the ability to differentiate between physical differences between different racial groups at about age three; racial orientation – from the age of five onwards the emergence of different feelings about each group; racial attitudes – the internalisation of stereotypes possibly leading to a more critical awareness and the understanding of racial differences. Katz (1973) developed this work by adding additional stages which are summarised below:

- The observation of racial cues which starts before the age of three, based on rudimentary observational cues and labels provided by adults.
- Conceptual differentiation which happens when children start to apply labels themselves and realise that skin colour is not the only determining feature of the concept; hair type and facial features are also included. Children test their ideas against adult feedback.
- The consolidation of group concepts and irrevocability of cues which happens before the age of five and describes the evaluative process of linking race and status and the beginning of the realisation that race does not change.
- Perceptual elaboration which occurs with children using concepts such as 'them' and 'us'.
- Cognitive elaboration that describes the influence of school, peers and other influences that add to attitudes about difference.
- Attitude crystallisation which occurs when individual attitudes are translated into action and become more resistant to change.

Photograph R1   Learning to respect each other

Practice example R1

Jude, a Year One teacher, was dismayed to hear the term 'Paki' used as a form of abuse by children in the playground. In discussion with colleagues and parents she decided to use a Persona Doll with her class in order to discuss the issues raised. Jude had been trained in the use of Persona Dolls for anti-bias strategies and had used them in the past in relation to disability. The doll was named Ibrahim, given a Pakistani Muslim identity, and used with the children for circle time discussions about Muslim culture and the effect of name-calling on Ibrahim.

Jude found that the children were very aware of the potential distress caused by negative attitudes and abusive behaviour and once the issues had been raised in a sympathetic and supportive environment were keen to talk about this. They were also aware of the negative use of the word 'Paki' although not all were fully aware of the racist implications of the term.

Jude used this discussion as a springboard for further class activities that celebrated and affirmed the diversity in the classroom and beyond the school gates. In consultation with the head teacher and other colleagues Jude helped to organise a team training day for the infant school staff, with an anti-racist focus. Eventually, these various activities were used to inform a review of the whole-school policy on name-calling and racism.

One of the most important findings is how early children can recognise and label racial differences. Ammons (1950) found that one in five two year olds and half of three year olds could distinguish skin colour and facial differences between black and white dolls. Milner also argues that it is hard to separate the learning of facts from the learning of feelings. Children as young as three may show an awareness of racial hierarchy 'in line with current adult prejudices' with white at the top and black at the bottom (Milner 1983: 108). In short it appears that where racism exists in the adult world, it is very likely that children will also learn negative attitudes.

Lane (2008) argues that a positive approach to difference is crucial not only for the individual child but also for the wider society which they will inherit. In her view (Lane 2008: 55) operating within a 'no-blame' culture and being able to discuss the issues in an atmosphere of mutual trust and understanding is a prerequisite for tackling racism effectively in early years provision and practice.

One of the challenges of implementing anti-racist strategies with young children is to ensure their full understanding and to encourage empathy and positive attitudes whilst acknowledging and addressing negative influences appropriately. Babette Brown (1999: 11) refers to this as a process of 'unlearning' the misinformation, stereotypes, discriminatory attitudes and behaviour that have already been learned. This is a journey we should all undertake if we are to eliminate racism and promote inclusive strategies in settings.

Refugees and asylum seekers

The legal definition of a refugee is a person who 'owing to a well-founded fear of being persecuted for reasons of race, religion, nationality, membership of a particular social group, or political opinion, is outside the country of his nationality, and is unable to or, owing to such fear, is unwilling to avail himself of the protection of that country' (UNHRC 1951).

An asylum seeker is someone who has applied for asylum and is waiting for a decision as to whether or not they are a refugee. In other words, in the UK an asylum seeker is someone who has asked the government for refugee status and is waiting to hear the outcome of their application.

According to the United Nations Refugee Agency in 2011, South Africa was the first destination for new asylum seekers with close to 107,000 new asylum claims and accounting for almost one-tenth of all individual applications worldwide. The next top receiving countries were the USA (76,000), France (52,100), Germany (45,700), Italy (30,300), Sweden (29,600) and Belgium (26,000). The UK was the eighth largest recipient of new asylum-seekers in 2011 with 25,455 applications (UNHRC 2011).

Tina Hyder writes emotively about the experience of being a refugee (2005: 26):

> Imagine yourself in this situation. You are the mother of four children, 11, 7, 5, and 2 years of age. You live in an area of the world that has experienced increasing political instability over the last few years. Civil unrest has recently erupted. Soldiers are now approaching your village and you know that you must gather your children and a few possessions and leave the village in the next hour. You will have to walk out into the mountains and so cannot carry very much. What do you feel? What do you tell your children? What few items do you decide to take with you?

Once arriving in the potential host country, often after arduous and dangerous journeys, for many refugees their situations are unlikely to improve. Hyder (2005) writes about the policy of dispersal in the UK which was introduced by the 1998 Asylum and Immigration Act. This policy has meant that families have often become isolated in areas where there might be very few people from their country of origin. In addition some host communities have been hostile and unsupportive. A briefing from the Information Centre about Asylum and Refugees (ICAR, Finney 2005) suggests that asylum seekers are often perceived as a threat and largely viewed to be economically motivated. The briefing highlights the role of the media in perpetuating negative attitudes and especially the tendency to use words like 'flood' or wave' when referring to immigration.

Research conducted by the Refugee Council and Save the Children (Rutter and Hyder 1998) highlighted the multiple issues of poverty, family separation, isolation and psychological trauma with which many families have to contend.

Practice example R2

Ashur, four years old, had just started in the nursery class at his local school. Little was known about the family except that they had recently left Syria after experiencing conflict there and had arrived in London because Ashur's uncle lived there. Ashur was very withdrawn and reluctant to socialise with other children. He has been found to be sensitive to loud noises and on one occasion had been found cowering under a table when a car outside backfired.

Ashur was immediately allocated a key worker who worked intensively to establish a trusting relationship. The key worker helped him to make an 'All about Me' book about himself in which he worked with her to provide captions for his drawings. He began to use small world play to act out some of his experiences and gradually became more relaxed in the company of the other children. Ashur's mother was invited to spend time with him in class and as a result made friends with another family in a similar situation to herself.

Olusoga (2008: 242) suggests that lack of appropriate information about the family background and experiences can be a hindrance to effective educational provision for children, but that the Early Years Curriculum with its room for emergent learning outcomes rather than prescribed pre-ordained learning objectives, is particularly suited to the needs of this group.

References

Ammons, R.B. (1950) Reactions in a projective doll-play interview of white males two to six years of age to differences in skin color and facial features, *Pedagogical Seminary and Journal of Genetic Psychology*, 6(2).

Brown, B. (1999) *Unlearning Discrimination in the Early Years*. Stoke-on-Trent: Trentham Books.

Coard, B. (1971) *How the West Indian Child is made Educationally Sub Normal in the British Education System*. London: New Beacon.

Derman-Sparks, L. (1989) *Anti-bias Curriculum: Tools for Empowering Young Children*. Washington, DC: National Association for the Education of Young Children.

Finney, N. (2005) *Key Issues: Public Opinion on Asylum and Refugee Issues*. www.icar.org.uk/briefing_attitudes.pdf (accessed 13 March 2013).

Goodman, M.E. (1964) *Race Awareness in Young Children*. New York: Collier Books.

Hyder, T. (2005) *War, Conflict and Play*. Maidenhead: Open University Press.

Katz, P.A. (1973) Perception of racial cues in pre-school children: a new look, *Developmental Psychology*, 8: 295–299.

Lane, J. (2008) *Young Children and Racial Justice*. London: National Children's Bureau.

Macpherson, W. (1999) *The Stephen Lawrence Inquiry: Report of an Inquiry by Sir William MacPherson of Cluny*. London: HMSO.

Milner, D. (1983) *Children and Race: Ten Years On*. East Grinstead: Ward Lock.

Olusoga, Y. (2008) Educating refugee children: a class teacher's perspective, in P. Jones, D. Moss, P. Tomlinson and S. Welch, (eds) *Childhood: Services and Provision for Children*. Harlow: Pearson Education.

Rutter, J. and Hyder, T. (1998) *Refugee Children in the Early Years: Issues for Policy-makers and Providers*. London: Save the Children and the Refugee Council.

UN Refugee Agency (UNHRC, 1951) *Convention and Protocol Relating to the Status of Refugees*. www.unhcr.org/3b66c2aa10.html (accessed 13 March 2013).

UN Refugee Agency (UNHRC, 2011) *Global Trends 2011: A Year of Crises*. www.unhcr.org.uk/fileadmin/user_upload/pdf/Global_Trends.pdf (accessed 13 March 2013).

S

Safety and risk

It is the clear responsibility of every early years setting that children and parents should feel safe both emotionally and physically within their provision. An inclusive setting is one where collective responsibility should be taken for safeguarding the well-being of all children and families who attend. At the same time we must acknowledge that there are many families and children in the UK today who, for a variety of reasons, do not feel safe and there may be little that practitioners can do in real terms to lessen these external risk factors and threats.

With the best will in the world no child or adult can be kept completely safe and secure from harm. Accidents, by nature, happen in unlikely and unforeseen of circumstances. In recent years writers such as Lindon (2011), Tovey (2007), Gill (2007) and Furedi (2002) have observed that an overemphasis on the avoidance of risk factors, especially with regard to outdoor, adventurous play, can have the unintended effect of narrowing or inhibiting children's learning and development, including their social skills, self-esteem and confidence. Lindon (2011) points out that a preoccupation with the avoidance of even very low-level risk can obscure our positive perceptions of the potential of certain learning and play activities and environments. In addition our fears and anxieties can be transmitted to the children themselves.

Tim Gill (2007) has described this approach as 'risk averse' whereby it is considered better not to take any chance at all in order to avoid being blamed for an accident. Tovey (2007: 5) points out the irony that: 'While children explore and navigate shrinking amounts of "real space" they can explore and navigate infinite amounts of "virtual space".' A certain amount of risk is essential if children are to learn the life

Photograph S1   Learning from first-hand experiences

skills necessary for survival. In addition we need to be aware of the extent to which our fears and concerns may be fuelled by sensationalised media stories or fear of litigation.

Lindon (2011: 5) makes a clear distinction between hazard and risk. She describes a 'hazard' as a physical situation that could be harmful to anyone. A risk is then the 'probability that the potential harm from this hazard will occur'. She describes the current shift from anxiety driven risk assessment towards risk benefit analysis as a positive step in which loss of potentially valuable experiences is also considered as part of the process. The complexity of the judgements that we have to make are exacerbated by the fact that what represented an unacceptable hazard for one child may be perfectly acceptable for another.

Photograph S2   Taking a leap

Stephenson (2003: 41) has pointed out that children naturally seek out and enjoy physical challenge and risk in their play. Furthermore she asserts that there may be 'a fundamental link between a young child's developing confidence in confronting physical challenges, and her confidence to undertake risks of quite different kinds in other learning contexts'.

Providing rich learning and experiences within safe limits is by no means an exact science. Particular challenges may arise when children cannot communicate effectively or lack a sense of danger. Dickins with Denziloe (2003: 13) make the point that disabled children are often overprotected from risk and effectively prevented from making their own choices. An inclusive approach to play and learning means that we should minimise the exclusion of children from any activities. Dickins et al. (2004) uses the example of climbing a tree to describe how it is possible to recreate the components of this experience for a child who is unable to experience it at first hand. For example, physical effort, being hidden from the world, looking down at people, the rustle of leaves, the texture and smell of bark and the wind on your face can be recreated for the child who cannot physically access this experience.

Practice example S1

At Mulberry Playgroup one of the privileges of being four years old is that you are allowed to help make the hot chocolate for the morning break. This includes stirring the pan at the stove, under appropriate adult supervision. This has become a very important ritual and privilege for the children. Joanne is epileptic and takes Epilim to control her symptoms which usually take the form of momentary absence seizures. One member of staff is unhappy about Joanna being allowed near the stove and wants her to be barred from this activity on the grounds of health and safety. After due consideration and in discussion with Joanna's mother staff decide that Joanne's self-esteem and confidence might suffer if she was treated differently from the other children and that this consideration over rides the risk that has been identified.

Ofsted (2006) has identified good practice in this area and observed that in outstanding settings an appropriate balance is achieved in which children can be adventurous, explore, make mistakes and take risks within safe limits. Furthermore the need for children to have the opportunity to take risks, in order to learn to be alert to potential dangers and keep themselves safe, is seen as fundamentally important.

Sensory impairment

A sensory impairment, as the name implies, is one which affects vision, hearing, taste, touch and sometimes spatial awareness. Of these conditions visual and hearing difficulties are the most common. Although these conditions are explored separately here, it is important to remember that some children will experience dual sensory impairment (deafblind) and that sensory impairments can combine with other difficulties to present a unique challenge for each individual child. Without intervention, sensory impairments can have an adverse effect on all areas of development, in particular the language acquisition process, conceptual development, motor development and behaviour.

A significant number of young children experience some degree of hearing difficulty, some of which may be temporary. Permanent hearing losses often result from damage to the cochlea or auditory nerve (sensori-neural deafness) and may vary from mild to profound. Conductive deafness describes deafness caused when sounds cannot pass efficiently through the outer and middle ear to the cochlea and auditory nerve. This can be because fluid in the middle ear makes it difficult for the three small bones in the middle ear to vibrate (usually known as glue ear); some part of the middle or outer ear has not formed properly and/or there is a blockage in the outer or middle ear. Most conductive deafness is temporary. It is usually caused by conditions like glue ear. This is very common among young children and will generally pass with time. There are often medical or surgical treatments that can improve this type of conductive deafness.

Some forms of conductive deafness are permanent. Some children are born without an ear canal, others may have no bones in their middle ear. The usual term for this is malformation of the ear. This means the ear has not formed as it would usually. There may not be any surgical or medical treatment to improve conductive deafness caused by this. When a child has sensori-neural deafness and a conductive hearing loss, it is described as mixed deafness or hearing loss. One example of a mixed hearing loss is when there is a temporary conductive deafness caused by a condition like glue ear as well as the permanent sensori-neural loss.

Another factor is that a child's hearing level can operate at different frequencies. It is possible to be deaf to the same level across all frequencies or to have different hearing levels at different frequencies. If a child has difficulty hearing sounds at higher frequencies, they may be described as having high-frequency deafness. If they have difficulty hearing sounds at low frequencies, they may be described as having low-frequency deafness. Frequency is very important when thinking about a child's ability to hear speech sounds. Different parts of speech happen at different frequencies.

Early detection of hearing loss is considered critical because there is such a strong relationship between hearing and language development. Indicators of a hearing loss in young children include failing to hear loud noises, difficulty in recognising the source of the sound and delayed language development.

Practice example S2

Rohan is three and a half and has just started at nursery. He is an only child and his mother explains that he has not socialised much with other children apart from his older cousins. Staff find that Rohan pays little attention to general instructions, especially when directed at the whole group, and is often very loud and noisy. During observations set up as part of putting together a behaviour plan the special educational needs coordinator (SENCo) observes that he does not respond when she stands behind him and talks. She suspects a hearing difficulty and approaches his mother with her concerns. With the help of the health visitor and speech therapist Rohan is identified as having a deteriorating hearing condition and given appropriate support including a hearing aid.

In early childhood there is a range of factors that can be responsible for a child becoming deaf. Infections like meningitis, measles and mumps can be a cause. Occasionally deafness is caused by an injury to the head or exposure to an extremely loud noise. Whatever the cause, early identification will be crucial.

Augmentative communication systems such as sign language or the use of communication boards (visual devices utilising pictures or symbols to represent communicative ideas) are often used with children who are hearing impaired. There are also various auditory assistive devices such as amplification systems and hearing aids.

There are various approaches to the development of speech and communication skills. Auditory-oral approaches aim to develop listening skills and spoken language in deaf children. They emphasise the importance of hearing aids, radio aids and cochlear implants to maximise the use of any hearing a deaf child has. Most auditory-oral approaches also use lip-reading to help the child's understanding. These approaches are used with children with all levels of deafness, from mild to profound. Auditory–oral approaches do not generally use sign language or finger spelling to support the understanding of spoken language. The main aim of these approaches is to allow deaf children to develop speech and communication skills so that they can communicate and mix with hearing people.

British Sign Language (BSL) is a visual language using hand shapes, facial expressions, gestures and body language to communicate. It has a structure and grammar different from that of written and spoken English. It is an independent and complete language with a unique vocabulary. Like other languages, it has developed over time and also has regional dialects. In March 2003 BSL was officially recognised as a language by the government. The aim of using a sign bilingual approach is to allow children to communicate using sign language and to develop skills in their home language. As BSL is a totally visual language being deaf need not affect a child's ability to learn the language. When they have become confident in BSL, they can use this as the medium to learn English. Using BSL also allows them access to the deaf community.

For many years the oral method of teaching was dominant and non-oral methods such as signing were often banned in schools and other institutions. The main aim of education was for children to communicate in English so that they would be able to communicate with their parents and peers. The argument that the cognitive development of deaf children proceeds better if it is underpinned by oral language is now questioned and many people argue that this led to the systematic underachievement of children with hearing impairments. Now BSL is in the ascendance and this has led to a discussion around whether deaf children might be better off in segregated schools with signing teachers and classmates. A report by the regulatory body, Ofsted (2012) highlighted the importance of trained teachers and specialist staff in supporting the best outcomes for deaf children in mainstream provision.

Many people in the deaf community resent the fact that so much time is spent helping children to vocalise, sometimes unsuccessfully, and in some schools signing is still banned. Many deaf people believe that signing is a language in its own right and that deaf people have the right to communicate in the way that they choose.

A sign bilingual approach uses sign language and the spoken language of the family. In the UK the two languages are usually BSL and English. If a family speaks another language in the home, such as Urdu or Bengali, then children may learn that as the second language with or without English.

Practice example S3

Siri is 18 months old and was born with visual and hearing impairment because her mother contracted the rubella virus in the early stages of her pregnancy. Staff in the nursery recognise that touch is an important sense for Siri and hold her close during group activities such as singing and story time. They use percussion instruments so that Siri can experience the vibrations and provide tactile play experiences such as finger-painting and allow her to experiment and play with her food at meal times. Staff are beginning to teach her simple Makaton signs in order to express her needs and have a multi-sensory environment in which Siri spends time every day.

Visual impairment can take many forms and may have varying implications for children's future development and achievements. The time of onset, for example, can be a crucial factor in the child's subsequent social and psychological adjustment. Total lack of vision (blindness) is very rare and most children have some degree of vision although it can be severely impaired. It is useful, for example, to find out if a child can distinguish light from dark and so on.

Various aspects of vision can be measured, for example, the ability to see fine detail (visual acuity), colour discrimination and movement perception; but if children are very young and/or non-verbal, pictures instead of letters or electrical measurement (using electrodes to send signals along visual pathways) may be used.

Different eye conditions create different ways of seeing: some pose difficulties with seeing things at a distance, others with seeing things that are near; some affect what a child can see clearly, others what they can see in their wider field of vision; some mean that children do not see in colour. Different visual conditions give rise to a range of effects, with different implications for each child. It is important to remember that each child is an individual and that even children with the same eye condition may appear to see very differently (Jennings 2009).

Children vary in the way they adapt and compensate for their visual loss by using and interpreting information from other senses. In general, they may have fewer opportunities to learn incidentally in the way that sighted children do. Skills which sighted children learn by imitation may need to be deliberately introduced to children who have a visual impairment.

Children who are visually impaired often experience delays in other areas of development. This is because vision can play a key role in reaching important milestones in early learning by giving children reliable information on which to construct their world. Another aspect is that because they cannot see what is available they may be less motivated to explore and manipulate than other children. A child with little or no vision has to make better use of other senses in order to make sense of their world and many visually impaired children will continue to explore objects orally or by tapping and banging for much longer than sighted children. Because children with visual impairments have difficulty seeing the non-verbal aspects of communication, such as eye contact and facial expression, they may experience speech and communication delay which in turn may effect social interaction. Motor difficulties are also common in children who are visually impaired.

For the reasons above, a child with any degree of visual impairment may not have the same range and variety of experiences as other children. For example, they may not participate as actively in the daily routines of eating, bathing and dressing which lead to independence. They may also be less sure of their ability to get about, which affects the way they interact with and negotiate the physical environment. Wilson (1998: 59) points out that one of the ways in which adults can help children with visual impairments to use their residual vision effectively is to actually limit the amount of assistance provided. She warns against 'learned helplessness' which can hinder children from independent exploration and movement.

Some adaptations may be necessary depending on the needs of the individual child. These might include handrails, lighting and contrast applications, and the removal of clutter and other hazards to provide safe access to different areas. Wilson recommends the provision of additional tactile, auditory and olfactory cues where necessary to support activities.

Focus on Foundation (RNIB 2001) emphasises practical considerations when working with visually impaired children. Visually impaired children respond better within an established consistent routine in an ordered environment. This should include taking account of the child's individual needs regarding lighting, sound levels and seating as advised by a qualified teacher of the visually impaired. Opportunities for spontaneous play with sensitive guidance will be an essential way of learning for a young child with visual impairment.

Practice example S4

Joey, who is two-and-a-half, has just started at nursery. He has had a slight visual impairment from birth, but in addition has also developed a condition called nystagmus which causes his eyes to look involuntarily from side to side rather than staying fixed on an object or person. Because his eyes are continually sweeping over what he is seeing it is difficult for him to obtain a clear image. He has rejected the glasses that have been prescribed for him to mitigate the effects of these impairments.

In order to help Joey settle in, staff create a quiet corner for him, keeping familiar toys within reach. Over time they gradually help Joey to establish routes to different parts of the setting but allowing him to retreat to his safe corner when he expresses the need. Staff also ensure that Joey has access to activities and toys that encourage his eyes to follow a moving object as well as those designed to develop hand–eye coordination. Over time they encourage and support Joey's growing independence and the development of positive relationships with peers.

Dickins with Denziloe (2003) point out that many disabled children need help to make the most effective use of their senses and recommend the use of multi-sensory environments and strategies which can ultimately benefit all children.

Practice example S5

Staff at Bright Futures nursery have three children attending the setting who have a range of sensory impairments. They decide to build a low-cost sensory environment and gradually accumulate useful items such as Christmas decorations, glittery fabrics, cushions, throws and lights. They choose a corner of the nursery that has blinds which exclude natural light and is relatively private. Once the area is assembled they play gentle music and birdsong and use aromatherapy to create a relaxing atmosphere. The area is very useful for calming and stimulating the children with sensory impairments and gradually becomes popular with all the children and even the staff.

Sexuality

This section deals with some of the issues raised by homophobic and heterosexist attitudes in early years settings. Kerry Robinson (2005: 177) has explored how the issue of sexuality and especially non-heterosexuality and young children has been taboo in the past and often seen as irrelevant to the lives of young children. Robinson refers to issues in society that make this an important and relevant aspect for those exploring equality and inclusion in relation to young children and their families 'The stark reality of an array of homophobic and heterosexist violence, hate crime murders and gay and lesbian adult and youth suicides clearly supports this claim.... Processes of prejudice, hatred and discrimination are well under way in the early years of children's lives'. She defines anti-homophobia and anti-heterosexist education as that which counters negative attitudes towards these issues and ensures that people in non-heterosexual relationships are not seen as deviant and abnormal. She stresses the importance of actively confronting negative attitudes and behaviour in early childhood because of the messages adults should be giving young children about all social injustices and breaches of individual rights.

Robinson (2005: 180) goes on to explore how addressing and confronting these issues in early childhood education will involve individuals confronting and examining their own prejudices and assumptions in just the same way that challenging racism involves self-scrutiny about our own bias: 'Thus, dealing with these issues can be confronting, unsettling and somewhat frightening at times, when deep personal biases, morals and often religious faiths are challenged'. However, she argues that this is a necessary step for early childhood educators to take, whatever their sexuality. After all you do not have to be Black to consider racism as an issue. She argues that it is crucial to provide children with the chance to 'critically deconstruct the inequities that exist in the world' (Robinson 2005: 184).

One of the earliest children's books to focus on the issue of gay parenting was *Jenny Lives with Martin and Eric,* written by Susanne Bosche and translated from Danish in 1983. Use of the book in a UK primary school resulted in a public furore and media backlash and there has been relatively little material targeting the early years since. Harding (2010: 84) examines the assumptions behind such media and public reactions:

- Teaching about same sex relationships is 'sex education'.
- It is not appropriate for institutions to teach young children about the existence of same sex (lesbian and gay) relationships.
- Young children are too innocent to attribute meaning to adult relationships and diverse relationship structures.
- Teaching about gay and lesbian relationships is running a gay agenda.

Harding goes on to examine each of these assumptions in turn, arguing that learning about relationships is not just about sex but about companionship and caring about each other. For Harding, failing to raise these issues will be failing to support children whose parents are in a same-sex relationship and she points out that young children will have already accrued ideas, some stereotypical, about adult relationships and they are not just 'innocent' in relation to these issues. She questions as to whether our 'squeamishness' about these issues is not just another manifestation of homophobia and heterosexism.

According to research by the campaigning charity Stonewall (Guasp 2009) more than two in five primary school teachers (44 per cent) say children experience homophobic bullying in their schools. A variety of reasons is given for this, most of which are unrelated to sexual orientation. Two in five primary school teachers hear children using homophobic language such as 'poof' or 'dyke'. Three-quarters of primary school teachers hear children use expressions such as 'that's so gay' or 'you're so gay'.

Any form of bullying is likely to have a significant negative effect on children's emotional and social well-being and even on their physical health. Social interaction and learning are also likely to be affected and children who are bullied are always in danger of becoming isolated. In the longer term this can lead to underachievement, truancy and school refusal. It has also been known to result in self-harm and even suicide as young people are unable to come to terms with the way they appear to be viewed by their peers and society in general.

Importantly, there is no evidence to suggest that, apart from the negative attitudes of others, having gay or lesbian parents is detrimental to the quality of family life or the experience of childhood. In fact a recent study (Bos and Gartrell 2010) found that children raised by lesbian mothers scored highly on measures of self-esteem and confidence, did better academically and were less likely to have behavioural problems such as rule-breaking and aggression.

Social class

The term social class is usually used to with reference to a group of people with similar levels of influence, wealth and status. The issue of social class is a complex one and sociologists typically use three methods to determine the boundaries. First, there is the objective method which measures and analyses 'hard' facts. Second, the subjective method asks people what they think of themselves. Third, the reputational method asks what people think of others.

Factors that are taken into account when determining an individual's social class will usually include: their education; the social background of their parents; their standard of living; their ownership of consumer durables; whether or not they own their own home; the value of their home if they do own it; their leisure pursuits; their accent and dress; their circle of friends and social connections; and their power and influence in society.

Class and poverty are generally considered to be interrelated yet separate. Whilst poverty is an experience that a person from any social background or class can undergo, class is often an important indicator of life chances and future wealth. All too often poverty can lead to deprivation and social exclusion where certain groups are more likely to be excluded from the benefits of mainstream society.

Economists, sociologists and political scientists all tend to perceive and define class in very different ways. For example, for many sociologists class is defined by occupational status related to employment. Economists, however, usually define class by income and political scientists are more likely to view and analyse class background in relation to ownership, power and control. Currently many UK government departments use categories and classifications based on occupational status but some government agencies and academics tend to use classifications based on socio-economic groups.

Typically social class has been subdivided into working class, middle class and upper class, although many observers agree that a new lower class or 'underclass' has emerged in society which is identified in terms of lack of education, poverty, homelessness and long-term unemployment (Jones 2011). Whilst there is clear evidence of social polarisation since the 1980s, arguably induced by government policies, there is still no conclusive proof that the groups affected by those policies are so detached from contemporary society that they should constitute a distinct class.

A recent study, known as *The Great British Class Survey*, was conducted by the Centre for Research on Socio-Cultural Change (CRSCC 2013). Seven categories were identified:

1. *Elite:* This is the most privileged class in Great Britain who have high levels of all three capitals (economic, cultural and social). Their high amount of economic capital sets them apart from everyone else.
2. *Established Middle Class:* Members of this class have high levels of all three capitals although not as high as the Elite. They are a gregarious and culturally engaged class.

3. *Technical Middle Class:* This is a new, small class with high economic capital but seem less culturally engaged. They have relatively few social contacts and so are less socially engaged.

4. *New Affluent Workers:* This class has medium levels of economic capital and higher levels of cultural and social capital. They are a young and active group.

5. *Emergent Service Workers:* This new class has low economic capital but has high levels of 'emerging' cultural capital and high social capital. This group are young and often found in urban areas.

6. *Traditional Working Class:* This class scores low on all forms of the three capitals although they are not the poorest group. The average age of this class is older than the others.

7. *Precariat:* This is the most deprived class of all with low levels of economic, cultural and social capital. The everyday lives of members of this class are precarious.

Vincent et al. (2007) make the point that people in the UK often deny class labels. For example, Jones (2011) makes the point that multi-millionaire business-man Mohamed Al Fayed once described himself as working class. Although this is an extreme example, many of us are confused about this issue. Jones points out that if you look at polling figures some people in the top socio-economic category do describe themselves as working class, but equally some in the bottom category think that they are middle class.

According to Blanden and Machin (2007) social mobility or the ability to tran-scend class boundaries in the UK remains at the low level it was for those born in 1970, with recent generations of children's educational outcomes still overwhelm-ingly tied to their parents' income. The report reviews evidence related to children born between 1970 and 2000 to determine whether the decline in social mobility between previous generations has continued. The main findings show that parental background continues to exert a powerful influence on the academic progress of chil-dren and that the UK remains stubbornly low in the international rankings of social mobility when compared with other advanced nations.

An important aim of anti-discriminatory and inclusive practice is that factors such as social class should never be a determinant of life chances or achievement for children. An early years experience that is free from exclusionary pressures and nega-tive and stereotypical attitudes is a vital first step along the road to social mobility.

References

Blanden, J. and Machin, S. (2007) *Recent Changes in Intergenerational Mobility in Britain.* www.lse.ac.uk/intranet/LSEServices/ERD/pressAndInformationOffice/PDF/ Recent%20Changes%20in%20Intergenerational%20Mobility%20in%20Britain.pdf (accessed 19 February 2013).

Bos, H. and Gartrell, N. (2010) Adolescents of the USA National Longitudinal Lesbian Family Study: can family characteristics counteract the negative effects of stigmatization, *Family Process*, 49(4): 559–572.

Bosche, S. (1983) *Jenny Lives with Eric and Martin*. London: Gay Men's Press.

Centre for Research on Socio-Cultural Change (CRSCC, 2013) *The Great British Class Survey*. www.cresc.ac.uk/our-research/trajectories-of-participation-and-inequality/the-great-british-class-survey (accessed 2 May 2013).

Dickins, M. with Denziloe, J. (2003) *All Together: How to Create Inclusive Services for Disabled Children and their Families. A Practical Handbook for Early Years Workers*. London: National Children's Bureau.

Dickins, M., Emerson, S. and Gordon-Smith, P. (2004) *Starting with Choice: Inclusive Strategies for Consulting Young Children*. London: Save the Children.

Furedi, F. (2002) *Culture of Fear: Risk Taking and the Morality of Low Expectations*. London: Continuum.

Gill, T. (2007) *No Fear: Growing up in a Risk Averse Society*. London: Calouste Gulbenkian Foundation.

Guasp, A. (2009) *Homophobic Bullying in Britain's Schools: The Teacher's Report*. London: Stonewall.

Harding, V. (2010) Too innocent to learn about two mums, in M. Guigni and K. Mundine (eds) *Talkin' up and Speaking Out*. Mt Victoria, NSW: Pademelon Press.

Jennings, J. (2009) *Including Children with Visual Difficulties in the Foundation Stage*. Bosworth: Featherstone Education.

Jones, O. (2011) *Chavs: The Demonization of the Working Class*. London: Verso.

Lindon, J. (2011) *Too Safe for Their Own Good? – Helping Children Learn About Risk and Lifeskills*. London: National Children's Bureau.

(Ofsted 2006) *Early Years: Safe and Sound. HMI 2663*. www.ofsted.gov.uk/resources/early-years-safe-and-sound-0 (accessed 6 February 2013).

(Ofsted 2012) *Communication is the Key. HMI 120169*. www.ofsted.gov.uk/resources/communication-key (accessed 25 March 2013).

Robinson, K. (2005) Doing anti-homophobia and anti-heterosexism in early childhood education: moving beyond the immobilising impacts of 'risks', 'fears' and 'silences'. Can we afford not to? *Contemporary Issues in Early Childhood*, 6(2): 175–188.

Royal National Institute for Blind People (RNIB, 2001) *Focus on Foundation: Including Children who are Blind or Partially Sighted in Early Years Setting*. London: RNIB.

Stephenson, A. (2003) Physical risk-taking: dangerous or endangered?, *Early Years*, 23(1): 35–43

Tovey, H. (2007) *Playing Outdoors*. Maidenhead: Open University Press.

Vincent, C., Braun, A. and Ball, S.J. (2007) *Childcare, Choice and Social Class: Caring for Young Children in the UK*. London: Institute of Education.

Wilson, R. (1998) *Special Educational Needs in the Early Years*. London: Routledge.

T

Teamwork

Successful inclusive practice always requires effective teamwork in order to develop and flourish. In order for teams to be successful, collaboration and cooperation will be vital (Giangreco 1997). Team members also need to share the same values and vision. Individual strengths must be valued and utilised and members will need to listen to each other effectively. A well-motivated and dynamic team usually enjoys challenge and demonstrates a willingness to solve problems as they arise.

From data gathered by Rodd (1998: 100–104) about how teamwork is usually understood by early years practitioners, a team was generally defined by Rodd (2006: 149) as: 'a group of people cooperating with each other to work towards achieving an agreed set of aims, objectives or goals while simultaneously considering the personal needs and interests of individuals'. Rodd also stressed the importance of shared values, ideals and vision. In order for inclusive approaches to be successful in settings and schools, a sense of common purpose and understanding will be needed in order to drive forward the agenda and to make the necessary changes and adjustments.

Being a team member is not always easy. A team is made up of individuals who each have their strengths, weaknesses, likes, dislikes, ideas and aspirations. For most of us it is important that we feel valued, involved, listened to and accepted. If team members are feeling excluded, devalued, controlled or disliked, then not only will their teamwork be inhibited but inclusion in the setting is unlikely to flourish. Although management and leadership issues are also vital, each team member carries responsibility for the success of a team. One of the challenges of team-focused management, however, is to harness the individual talents, qualities, skills, knowledge and experience effectively. Teams that are able to discuss the issues and challenge which arise openly, honestly and respectfully are more able to work collaboratively.

For the last ten years UK government legislation and guidance has emphasised the Every Child Matters agenda (DfES 2003) with the goal of integrated services at its heart. For early years providers this development has brought recognition that they are also part of a wider team that is working in the best interests of the children in their care. Members of the wider team will come from a range of disciplines such as health visitors, social workers, educational psychologists, speech therapists, physiotherapists, advisory teachers and community police officers. Just one of the challenges of working together effectively is that professionals from the various disciplines may not agree on values, approaches and philosophies and they may also bring with them a different language with different meanings and understanding around the shared issues and situations with which they are confronted. According to Rodd (2006) such differences have effectively prevented the development of a partnership approach in the past.

The development of Sure Start and the Children's Centre programme has been the biggest manifestation, so far, of a collaborative approach to service provision. The development of the Common Assessment Framework (CAF) for assessing children and families in need was also an attempt to share values and principles in the best interest of children and families.

Practice example T1

Ivana, who is two-and-a-half, has cerebral palsy, which means that she finds it difficult to walk, and a hearing impairment that has just been identified. Her family is known to have housing difficulties and are in temporary accommodation. Staff at the nursery, in consultation with Ivana's parents, decide that a CAF assessment would be the best way to meet the family's needs.

A Team Around the Child (TAC) is drawn together which includes Ivana's parents and key worker at the nursery; a physiotherapist, health visitor, educational psychologist, family social worker and the setting special educational needs coordinator (SENCo) who is appointed lead professional by the team. An action plan is put together which includes a formal assessment of Ivana's difficulties and a review of the family circumstances.

Team members meet regularly with the family to ensure that the views of the family are taken account of. A family support plan is drawn up which takes account of the kind of care and support Ivana will need to access play and learning in the setting and prioritises the housing needs of the family.

In many parts of the UK the Team Around the Child (TAC) approach (Siraj-Blatchford et al. 2007) has gained acceptance as a way of coordinating early interventions for young children who have multiple or complex needs and need long-term practical intervention on a regular basis from a number of practitioners.

Each TAC should have a multi-agency membership which brings together the key practitioners who support the child regardless of who they work for. It should empower parents by offering them a full place in the team and have a team leader with a very clearly defined and limited role who functions as the multi-agency key worker for the child and family. A TAC can include teachers, therapists, early years practitioners, health visitors, nurses, social workers, portage workers, social workers and others. One function of each TAC is to appoint a lead professional whose role is to act as a single point of contact for the child or family, coordinate the delivery of the actions agreed by the practitioners involved, and reduce overlap and inconsistency in the services offered to families. The lead professional may be based in any sector of the children, young people or family workforce, depending on the issues involved and the individual relationship with the child.

Whether a team is based in an individual setting or is part of a wider professional network, they will need to agree on a purpose, code of conduct, protocol and procedures, vision, values, roles and responsibilities as early as possible. A team that has agreement on these issues can more easily ensure that its efforts are purposeful and that all members contribute effectively.

Terminology

It is sometimes difficult to know what terms/words to use when we are talking about issues that are considered sensitive or taboo such as disability, sexuality and race. Some people may feel so anxious or unsure about using the 'correct' or 'right' word or term that they consequently try to avoid using them at all. Yet most of us would agree that what people call us and how they refer to us is of fundamental importance to our self-esteem and identity as individuals.

The reality is that there are few absolutely 'correct/right' or 'incorrect/wrong' words except where the intention is to hurt, to discriminate or to abuse. If there is no such intention we need to be particularly sensitive about our approach and the language that we use. It is unlikely that people working with young children would use overtly offensive words to describe people or situations. But some people may unwittingly use terms that others find unacceptable or inappropriate, although they are in no way intended to have this effect.

Practice example T2

Patrick's grandmother brings him to nursery three days a week. A member of staff overhears her referring to a group of boys as 'coloured chappies'. She takes her aside and explained that many Black people find this term offensive. The grandmother apologises and explains that she meant no harm. She promises to be careful how she refers to people in future.

The term 'special educational need', for example, came into common usage after the Warnock Report (DES 1978) which examined in great detail the provision then available and made key recommendations that informed subsequent legislation and significantly changed provision. The term was considered less stigmatising and a useful euphemism for terms like 'handicapped' and 'subnormal' that were applied to describe children at the time (DES 1978: 37). Ironically, this term has for some time been itself under scrutiny as the notion that someone is 'special' marks them out from others and implies that they do not have 'ordinary' needs, entitlements and aspirations. It also has very general applications, which can include children with disabilities and impairments, children with emotional and behavioural difficulties, those with mental health problems, and so on. Many people believe that the term has so many applications that it ceases to be helpful. The term 'additional needs' is increasingly used as an attempt to overcome some of these problems, but it is still very general and likely to objectify and set children apart from their peers.

Terminology is always changing. What may have been acceptable at one time may no longer be so. Crucially we need to talk with others about the words and terms we use. We need to reflect on and consider their meanings, be receptive to change and recognise that other people may have different understandings. We may find that there is a lack of agreement between certain groups and individuals about how they should be described and what they should be called. Rather than feeling guilty or apprehensive about the words we use, we should talk with other people and ask those involved or affected what they wish to be called and which words they feel comfortable with.

Travellers and Gypsies

Gypsies and Travellers are a long-established group in Britain whose histories and tradition go back hundreds of years. The Gypsy and Traveller population is made up of English Romani Gypsies and Travellers, Welsh Gypsies, Scottish Gypsy-Travellers and Irish Travellers, smaller groups of Roma from Central and Eastern Europe and also 'New' Travellers and Circus Travellers (Cemlyn and Clark 2005).

Romany Gypsies and Irish Travellers are recognised as distinct ethnic groups in terms of anti-discriminatory legislation in the UK. It is difficult to establish the number of UK Gypsies and Travellers as they are not currently identified as a separate ethnic group in the census. No reliable figures exist for the number of Gypsies and Travellers who live in conventional housing.

According to a study by Sheffield University (Parry et al. 2004) Gypsy Travellers have significantly poorer health status and significantly more self-reported symptoms of ill health than other UK residents, including English-speaking minority ethnic groups and economically disadvantaged White UK residents. Using standardised measures as indicators of health, Gypsy Travellers have poorer health than that of their age- and sex-matched comparators. Self-reported chest pain, respiratory problems and arthritis were also more prevalent in the Traveller group. For Gypsy Travellers, living in a house is associated with long-term illness, poorer health state and anxiety. Those who rarely travel have the poorest health.

Cemlyn and Clark (2005) examined the plight of Gypsies and Travellers in relation to poverty and social exclusion which they regard as multidimensional. They cite deprivation of activities considered customary such as attending school, poor living conditions and lack of basic amenities, especially given the lack of authorised sites across the country. They also describe 'a spatial element' to their social exclusion because of this lack of secure accommodation, safety and access to services. They regard Gypsies and Travellers as essentially excluded from society as evidenced not only by public behaviour and attitudes, but also by institutional policies and service provision.

According to a study by Wilkin et al. (2009: 40) Gypsy and Traveller children in particular face the following challenges:

> Overall lack of suitable accommodation, insufficient or poorly maintained sites and the threat of eviction have all been identified in the literature as impacting on the physical well-being of Gypsy Traveller children and young people. Every Child Matters (ECM) promotes the safety of all children from accidental injury, maltreatment and neglect (HM Government, 2004), yet most Traveller sites lack safe play areas for children and even the most basic fire-fighting.
>
> Racism has been found to adversely affect children's well-being and confidence, as have medical absences from school which may signal psychosocial stress, although this might not always be recognised by school. Traveller pupils are reported to employ a range of coping strategies to deal with racism including avoidance, retaliation and hiding their identity.

Practice example T3

Some staff at Penfold Nursery expressed alarm when they heard that two settled Irish Traveller families had applied for places for their children. At a staff meeting fears were expressed that the children might be neglected and unmanageable and that their attendance might deter other families from applying. The nursery manager was aware that turning the families away would be discriminatory under equalities legislation. She contacted the local authority Traveller Education Liaison Officer who came and gave a talk to parents and staff about Traveller culture and the problems these families had faced prior to becoming settled. Some parents expressed surprise at the positive aspects of Traveller culture, such as a strong cultural identity and the emphasis that was put on cleanliness and codes of behaviour.

Staff brought positive resources such as pictures and puzzles and one staff member used a Persona Doll to talk to the children about Traveller life. When the children started nursery they struggled with routine but after a while they settled down and started to enjoy nursery life.

A report published in 2006 by the University of Birmingham (Mason et al. 2006) recommended that work with service providers and policymakers needed to be adequately resources and maintained over time. They also highlighted the lack of effective links between those who were involved with service provision and those responsible for broader policies. Significantly they concluded that work with children and families needed to be underpinned by an acceptance on the part of local authorities of their duties and responsibilities towards the Gypsy and Traveller community.

Lane (2008) emphasises the importance of including Gypsy and Traveller groups explicitly in setting policies and that the provision of appropriate and positive resources which reflect Traveller culture should be a priority whether or not children are currently attending.

References

Cemlyn, S. and Clark, C. (2005) The social exclusion of gypsy and traveller children, in G. Preston (ed.) *At Greatest Risk: The Children Most Likely to be Poor.* London: Child Poverty Action Group.

Department for Education and Science (DES, 1978) *Special Educational Needs (The Warnock Report). Report of the Enquiry into the Education of Handicapped Children and Young People.* London: HMSO.

Department for Education and Skills (DfES, 2003) *Every Child Matters.* London: HMSO.

Giangreco, M.F. (1997) Key lessons learned about inclusive education: summary of the 1996 Schonell Memorial Lecture, *International Journal of Disability, Development and Education,* 44(3): 193–206.

Lane, J. (2008) *Young Children and Racial Justice.* London: National Children's Bureau.

Mason , P., Plumridge, G., Barnes, M., Beirens, H. and Broughton, K. (2006) *Preventative Services for Gypsy/Traveller Children: A Final Report of the National Evaluation of the Children's Fund.* Birmingham: University of Birmingham.

Parry, G., Van Cleemput, P., Peters, J., Moore, J., Walters, J., Thomas, K. and Cooper, C. (2004) *The Health Status of Gypsies and Travellers in England: Summary of a Report to the Department of Health.* Sheffield: University of Sheffield.

Rodd, J. (1998) *Leadership in Early Childhood: The Pathway to Professionalism.* Sydney: Allen & Unwin.

Rodd, J. (2006) *Leadership in Early Childhood.* Maidenhead: Open University Press.

Siraj-Blatchford, I., Clarke, K. and Needham, M. (2007) *The Team Around the Child: Multi-agency Working in the Early Years.* Stoke-on-Trent: Trentham Books.

Wilkin, A., Derrington, C. and Foster, B. (2009) *Improving the Outcomes for Gypsy, Roma and Traveller Pupils.* London: DCSF.

U

Underachievement
Unique child
United Nations Convention on the Rights of the Child (UNCRC)

Underachievement

Underachievement can be defined as an inability or failure of an individual child or group of children to perform in accordance with their age or talents. Research indicates that there are many children in the UK who do not achieve their full potential in educational or life terms. The underpinning issues are complex and the temptation to generalise or predict about particular groups should be resisted, as low expectations contribute to poor outcomes for children. An inclusive setting will set out to ensure that every unique and individual child does as well as they can in order to lead full and satisfying lives.

Statistics from the Foundation Stage Profile Results for England for 2007–08 showed that girls continue to outperform boys in all 13 assessment scales. The gap appears particularly wide in social and emotional development, literacy, writing and creative development.

A report from the Joseph Rowntree Foundation in 2007 (Casses and Kingdon 2007) found that the great majority of low achievers are White and British, and there are far more boys than girls. Many of them come from disadvantaged backgrounds where there is a high unemployment rate. Low achievers are commonly to be found in poor urban areas, but there are considerable variations between comparable local authority areas. Some schools with high proportions of disadvantaged pupils do much better than others and there is also a wide range of performance among different ethnic groups. This report stressed the importance of a positive and productive early years experience in enabling children to overcome disadvantage.

White British pupils were found to be more likely than other ethnic groups to persist in low achievement. If they started in the lowest categories of achievement in primary school, they were more likely than other ethnic groups to remain there at the end of secondary school.

Children with special educational needs comprise an unacceptably high propor-tion of low achievers and studies have shown that more could be done to assist them through their schooling. The same is true of looked after children. Whilst educational achievement is only one aspect of children's lives, it is the experience of failure and the subsequent impact on self-esteem and identity that can be especially damaging.

Siraj-Blatchford (2010) collected individual case studies that aimed to investigate children and their families who succeeded against the usual 'odds' of disadvantage. The EPPE project had previously found that although parents' levels of education were significantly related to child outcomes, the quality of the home learning envi-ronment was the most important. When case study parents were asked what they felt were the barriers to providing a positive home learning environment they cited time and family pressures and personal circumstances such as health. The study also found that disadvantaged families very often have high aspirations for their children and many provide significant educational support, although the cost of additional activities and outings, etc. may be prohibitive for some. Siraj-Blatchford (2010: 477) observes:

> When parents are aware that their child has as much potential as any other to be successful, and when they recognize that they have an active role to play themselves in realizing this potential, then early social disadvantages may be overcome.

The implications are that a can-do approach for children coupled with a positive approach to working with families that supports their existing strengths and values their efforts is more likely to be successful in improving educational outcomes for children than one which stigmatises and blames parents for their perceived short-comings and failings.

Unique child

The principle of the Unique Child is enshrined in both the original Early Years Foun-dation Stage blueprint and the revised 2012 version. This principle celebrates the uniqueness of every child and urges practitioners to take the time to observe, listen and tune in, in order to understand what it is that makes each child tick. As children's strengths, interests, preferences and different developmental pathways and learning possibilities begin to unfold, practitioners can plan responsively to capture and design experiences that are meaningful to children and tailored to individual needs. This con-cept of each child as a unique and valuable individual is central to inclusive approaches and thinking because of the way it encourages us to value and respect the differences between us as human beings and to consider children and family perspectives.

In 2010 researchers from Sheffield Hallam University (Garrick et al. 2010) con-ducted research to explore children's perspectives about their experiences of the Early

Years Foundation Stage (EYFS). Researchers worked with 146 children aged between three and five in different types of early years settings across four local authorities in England. When asked about how well early years settings met individual needs and interests, children were generally positive about their experiences. In addition Garrick et al. (2010: 5) found that:

- Children especially appreciated social play opportunities, social occasions and opportunities to care for others in their settings.
- Children's views reflected their need for parents, carers and siblings to be welcomed into settings.
- Children talked about variations in how far adults get to know them as individuals. Children's comments suggested that in smaller settings they were more likely to feel that adults knew them as individuals.
- Children demonstrated great interest in the rules, boundaries and routines of their settings. Some children seemed to find this structure helpful; others seemed to want more freedom. Children were often keen to understand why particular rules and routines were needed.

One of the most important aspects of recognising the principle of the unique child is the avoidance of stereotyping. A stereotype is usually understood as a fixed or over-generalised belief about a group or class of people. Stereotypical ideas can be damaging because they bring with them assumptions about people that may have little basis in reality. Children from all sorts of minority groups are particularly vulnerable to stereotyping because practitioners and others may have preconceived and/or fixed ideas about who they are, what their needs might be, and how they are likely to behave. Gender stereotyping is also common because of deeply held cultural beliefs about masculinity, femininity and what might be considered desirable traits and behaviour for boys and girls. Golombok and Fivush (1994) makes the point that racial, ethnic and economic stereotypes combine with gender stereotypes to produce complex patterns of belief about groups of people.

Practice example U1

A practitioner in a nursery in Bradford wanted to overcome the stereotype expressed by her colleagues that young Asian girls are generally passive and restrained in their play. She organised a series of outings to local outdoor spaces ensuring that the girls had access to activities such as climbing, running and building a den. Afterwards she found that the girls were much more likely to engage in active and boisterous play in the setting once they knew that this behaviour was permissible and the opportunities for them to take part in these activities had been ensured.

United Nations Convention on the Rights of the Child (UNCRC)

It is possible that few of the positive changes to early years principles, policy and practice over the last 20 years would have taken place without the underpinning of the United Nations Convention of the Rights of the Child 1989 to ensure commitment and to drive forward the global agenda for all children. In 1923 Egalantyne Jubb, the founder of Save the Children, summarised what she believed to be essential rights that all children should have. These points formed the basis of the Declaration on the Rights of the Child agreed by the general assembly of the International Save the Children Union in 1923.

A year later the League of Nations adopted these points, which were then known as the Declaration of Geneva. The Universal Declaration of Human Rights, adopted in 1948, included children in its remit but it was not seen to safeguard the specific rights of children. In 1959 the UN General Assembly adopted the Declaration on the Rights of the Child but it was not until the 1980s that serious debate took place about what the nature of children's rights should be (Wyse and Hawtin 2000).

The UNCRC sets out from the premise that everyone has rights, including children, but that children, owing to their age and lack of power, are more likely to have their rights ignored and forgotten. The UK government signed up to the document in 1991 which means that UK law and the way(s) in which children are treated in the UK must meet the standards set out in the convention. The USA and Somalia were the only countries not to ratify the convention.

The Convention sets out a number of statements called Articles which state the rights that all children and young people up to the age of 18 should have. These rights apply to children and young people regardless of where they live or the economic status of the countries in which they live. In addition the Convention serves to remind us that the promotion of the rights of children should be an international concern across all disciplines. There are three main rights which must be considered whenever decisions are made about children (UNICEF 2013):

> *Non-discrimination*: Article 2 states that all rights in the convention apply to all children whatever their sex, race, religion, disability, opinion or family background.
>
> *Best interests*: Article 3 states that whenever adults or organisations make decisions which affect children, they must always think first about the best interests of the child.
>
> *Children's views*: Article 12 states that children have a right to say what they think about anything that affects them and must be listened to carefully. Courts and official bodies must also listen to children's viewpoints when making decisions which affect children.

By its very nature all of the Articles of the UNCRC promote equality and inclusion but particularly relevant to the issues under scrutiny regarding disabled children are Article 6 which states that children have a right to life and to the best possible chance to develop fully, and Article 23 which states that disabled children must be helped to be as independent as possible.

There are many other rights given to children in the convention (UNICEF 2013): the right to become a citizen of a particular country (Article 7); the right to freedom of thought and religion (Article 14); the right to personal privacy (Article 16); and the right to be protected from violence and harmful treatment (Articles 19 and 37). In addition children are given economic, social, cultural and protective rights, e.g. the right to health care (Article 24), and the right to a free education up to primary school level (Article 28).

The government has to send the UN Committee on the Rights of the Child a report every five years explaining how children's rights are being consolidated and put into practice (Wyse and Hawtin 2000). An independent organisation called the Children's Rights Alliance for England monitors the implementation.

Alderson (2000: 23) makes the point that children's rights are 'limited 'in that they concern freedoms and obligations which can be deliberately delivered or withheld'. She describes some rights which might be considered aspirational according to each nation's available resources. Rights are also conditional in that in exercising their own rights people must also accept responsibilities and obligations to the state and to others.

The UN Committee examined the UK government in 1995, 2002 and in 2008. The most recent report (UNCRC 2008) includes over 120 recommendations for action needed to improve children's lives, many of which made specific reference to children's participation rights and placed particular emphasis on the rights of disabled children to take part in decision making. They also recommended that the UK government should raise the age at which criminal law applies to children and make a law that makes the physical punishment of children illegal.

The UN Committee felt that the UK had made 'little progress to enshrine Article 12 in education law and policy' and that the 'participation of children in all aspects of schooling is inadequate'. The UN Committee also criticised the 'insufficient action' to 'ensure the rights enshrined in Article 12 to children with disabilities'. The next examination of the UK is scheduled for 2014.

In 2001 the post of Children's Commissioner for Wales was created by the Children's Commissioner for Wales Act 2001, to safeguard and promote the rights and welfare of children, using the UNCRC to guide the work. Subsequent legislation created a Children's Commissioner for Northern Ireland (The Commissioner for Children and Young People (NI) Order 2003), Scotland (Commissioner for Children and Young People (Scotland) Act 2003) and England (sections 1–9 of the Children Act 2004)(Great Britain Parliament 2003a, 2003b, 2004). The English Commissioner is unique in the UK in not having the remit to promote children's rights.

In 2010 an independent review was undertaken of the role of the English Commissioner (Dunford 2010). The report criticised the limited role of the Children's

Commissioner and called for greater independence from government and increased powers to assess the impact of new policies on the rights of children. Wyse (2004) links the relative lack of progress in the UK to historical attitudes towards children and childhood.

Although the rights of children are often marginalised or ignored by societies, especially those in the grip of poverty, conflict or economic downfall, the UNCRC is a vital instrument which plays an important role in reminding governments and individuals of their moral and ethical duties towards all children.

References

Alderson, P. (2000) The rights of young children, in H. Penn (ed.) *Early Childhood Services: Theory, Policy and Practice.* Buckingham: Open University Press.

Casses, R. and Kingdon, K. (2007) *Tackling Low Educational Achievement.* York: Joseph Rowntree Foundation.

Dunford, J. (2010) *Review of the Office of the Children's Commissioner (England).* www.education.gov.uk/publications/eOrderingDownload/Cm-7981.pdf (accessed 10 February 2013).

Garrick, R., Bath, C., Dunn, K., Maconochie, H., Willis, B. and Wolstenholme, C. (2010) Children's Experiences of the Early Years Foundation Stage. www.gov.uk/government/uploads/system/uploads/attachment_data/lile/182163RR071.pdf (accessed 22 July 2013).

Golombok, S. and Fivush, R. (1994) *Gender Development.* Cambridge: Cambridge University Press.

Great Britain Parliament (2004) *Children Act 2004* (c.145). London: HMSO.

Great Britain Parliament (2003a) *Commissioner for Children and Young People (NI) Order 2003.* www.legislation.gov.uk/nisi/2003/439/contents/made (accessed 10 February 2013).

Great Britain Parliament (2003b) Commissioner for Children and Young People (Scotland) Act 2003. www.legislation.gov.uk/asp/2003/17/contents (accessed 10 February 2013).

Siraj-Blatchford, I. (2010) Learning in the home and at school: how working class children 'succeed against the odds', *British Educational Research Journal,* 36(3): 463–482.

United Nations Convention on the Rights of the Child (UNCRC, 2008) *Concluding Observations.* www2.ohchr.org/english/bodies/crc/docs/AdvanceVersions/CRC.C.GBR.CO.4.pdf (accessed 10 February 2013).

United Nations Children's Fund (UNICEF, 2013) www.unicef.org/crc/ (accessed 19 May 2013).

Wyse, D. (2004) *Childhood Studies: An Introduction.* Oxford: Blackwell.

Wyse, D. and Hawtin, A. (eds) (2000) *Children: A Multi-Professional Perspective.* London: Arnold.

V

Voices of practitioners

In 2005–6 the Early Childhood Unit at the National Children's Bureau held a series of conferences around England designed to allow practitioners, managers and advisory staff to consider issues of inclusion within mainstream early years settings. The conference agenda was designed around the Early Childhood Forum definition of inclusion that has also been adopted as a key approach for this book.

As part of the activities, participants were asked to consider what they felt represented the current barriers to inclusive practice in the settings for which they were responsible (Owen 2006). There was complete agreement in all of the groups about the underpayment and undervaluing of childcare workers and the effect this has on skill levels, confidence and the ability to think creatively about inclusive practice. It was felt that this was an issue that was not being tackled nationally and that some barriers will not be overcome until the value and status of practitioners is addressed. Some of the replies are considered below because they so accurately encapsulate the difficulties and challenges. In order for any setting to become inclusive it is essential that there are opportunities for the voices and opinions of practitioners to be heard. One of the emerging themes was that of training. Below are some typical comments:

> 'Key barriers are the cost and availability of training, it is too expensive for early years settings, especially in PVI [private, voluntary, independent] sector, and often not appropriate to their needs.'

> 'The private sector has specific problems with settings not having such ready access to training or the resources to release staff.'

> 'Senior managers need to attend relevant training, not just front line staff.'

'To work, training really needs to be part of a continuous process of self-review, ideally settings should be able to train together.'

'Training is only effective if disseminated to staff team or if the whole team is trained together.'

'Often it's hard to get people out to training, especially if it's branded as equal opportunities or equalities because they think they've already covered it.'

'There is a lack of systematic mechanisms for transferring knowledge and skills.'

'We haven't built up a consistent enough body of work on this or got it recognised within the qualifications system.'

Significantly, participants expressed a desire for appropriate training that raised awareness of issues and addressed negative attitudes. For many, although one-day delegate training was useful, their needs around the issues of equality and inclusion were for whole team training that included managers and encouraged a change of ethos. Practitioners also felt that the ability and opportunity to share knowledge and skills between settings was vital in order to raise awareness and build expertise. The cost of training and the difficulty of finding and financing staff for cover were all highlighted as significant barriers.

Another significant issue that arose was the importance of having shared values and a sense of purpose:

'Staff attitudes can be very varied and for a setting to have an inclusive approach everyone needs to be working to the same principles and practices.'

'Even when settings have inclusion or equalities policies they are sometimes not known or understood by all staff and may be irrelevant to that settings because brought in from somewhere else.'

'Settings need to see the bigger picture, being proactive, not reactive.'

'Too often there is a lack of a shared sense of responsibility for all children in a setting or for the community the setting is in.'

Generally the issue of targets was felt to be problematic in relation to developing and maintaining inclusive practice:

'There is a tension between setting stretching targets for children of particular ages and the inclusion of children who are not going to achieve those targets.'

'There are some excellent schools which are just getting on with the job of educating all their children, but this is not recognised because they are not heading league tables.'

'These days there is more pressure on parents for their children to "achieve" at this age rather than being able to develop through play at their own pace, it sets up tensions.'

'League tables work against inclusive policies.'

'Staff in "education" settings are not always encouraged to recognise that caring for children's physical needs is part of their job.'

'There are too many targets and they're different for different sectors so people have trouble working with each other, also lots of structural changes in PCTs and local authorities mean that it's hard to get a consistent line on things like inclusion policies.'

Many practitioners who participated expressed the challenges of working effectively with parents, particularly with regard to disabled children and those for whom English is not a first language:

'It's difficult to draw the balance between meeting parents' and children's needs, children don't always benefit when meeting parents' needs.'

'There can be a lack of will to include parents because it's another whole area of work to take on board.'

'Some parents refuse to accept a label for their child because they see it as stigmatising, while others welcome it because it helps them understand their child's difficulties.'

Some parents are over-protective and don't allow the staff to meet the children's needs.'

'It is difficult for staff to challenge discrimination and stereotypes with parents, there need to be more forums for open discussion.'

'Additional language learning brings lots of tensions, for instance staff may be encouraging parents to speak English while also stressing that it's good for children to retain their first language. They need to be very good communicators in order to explain the work of the setting in this and other respects.'

Effective leadership and management were felt to be crucial in order to make a real difference in settings:

> 'You need a manager with the right attitude, who can get at least 50 per cent of the staff enthusiastic about the change and you need to be clear about the role before rushing out and offering services, a focused approach rather than crisis management.'

> 'Leaders have to take responsibility for this issue, to want to look at it and be able to deal with it.'

Some participants felt that a lack of effective multi-agency working was a barrier:

> 'Where it takes three months for responsible agencies to identify and allocate additional help, it is difficult for settings to give an unambiguous, welcoming "Yes" when families first knock on the door, looking for placement.'

> 'There is a need to focus on the child and the family's needs rather than on the service or the agency's systems.'

Another clear theme identified was a general lack of political will both at government and local authority level alongside concerns about how inclusive practice is regulated:

> 'Strategic planning rarely focuses on inclusion and is often reactive rather than proactive.'

> 'There needs to be coherence in legislation and in policy nationally and a common understanding and acceptance of their responsibility for this by local authorities.'

> 'Ofsted have clout but no expertise, we need local authority expertise and Ofsted clout to come together.'

> 'Some local authorities are doing a lot and others very little, we need more standard expectations and procedures at national level, for instance in data collection which is often inconsistent, health agencies are even a barrier to collecting data in some situations.'

It is clear that many of the issues raised by practitioners here have still to be addressed. Their comments are particularly poignant because the level of local authority support in many areas is likely to dwindle due to cuts in services and changes in government policy. However, listening to practitioners and incorporating their views and experiences remains an essential part of working towards more effective inclusive practice for all children and families.

Reference

Owen, S. (2006) *Participation and Belonging: Report of a Series of Conferences on Inclusion in Early Years Settings*. London: National Children's Bureau.

W

Well-being

Well-being

The concept of well-being for children is integral to the aims and objectives of inclusive practice. An inclusive setting should be concerned about the well-being of all its members. While there is no agreed definition of well-being, there is a consensus that it draws in the many different factors which affect children's lives including material conditions, housing and community, how children feel and achieve in education, their health, exposure to risks, and the quality of relationships and the ways in which they develop. Waters (2009: 17) observes that, according to a systematic review of the child well-being literature, the definition of child well-being is highly variable and that the general understanding of the term usually relates to being 'comfortable', 'healthy' and 'happy'.

From a theoretical perspective well-being is often perceived of as an individual characteristic. Anning and Edwards (2006: 55) refer to it as a 'within person' characteristic. This understanding is often prevalent in UK policy and literature. From this perspective an individual can have a sense of well-being regardless of the well-being of other individuals, family or community. Some international perspectives and theorists, however, take as their premise that well-being is a social concept in which the well-being of the group is paramount. Bronfenbrenner (1979), for example, argued that the realisation of human abilities is largely dependent on social and institutional context. He believed therefore that it was not only the individual child that needed attention and support but also the caregivers. Roberts (2010: 19) asserts that 'a child's well-being is determined by the level of parental, familial, communal and social wellness'.

Historically, well-being has often been linked to health. The World Health Organization (WHO 1948) uses the concept of well-being to describe the 'global' health of a person. Pollard and Lee (2002) suggest that there are five distinct domains of well-being that are to be found in the literature. There is the physical domain which includes many issues that are reflected in policy concerns, such as rates of growth and obesity, healthy eating and staying safe. The psychological domain refers to psychosocial issues such as self-esteem, confidence and emotional well-being as well as overall mental health. The cognitive domain covers aspects that are intellectual and includes how children feel about themselves in relation to their academic performance. The social domain relates to communication skills, the availability of emotional and practical support as well as sociological perspectives such as family and peer relationships. Finally, the economic domain includes access to and availability of economic support such as government benefit systems. Other factors included are family income and wealth and economic hardships and deprivation. Whilst each of these domains may underpin potential well-being it is important to remember that they are not mutually exclusive and there is likely to be a complex interplay of factors that underpin the well-being of any individual child.

Whilst it is clear that enhancing children's lives and improving child well-being should be a central objective of future children's policy and practice, it is also increasingly clear that well-being is a complex concept that may have different meanings to the wide range of professionals who work with young children.

Every Child Matters and all recent legislation and guidance reflect the current concern in UK society about the well-being of children. In 2007 a UNICEF report compared overall child well-being across material well-being, health and safety, education, peer and family relationships, behaviours and risks, and young people's own subjective sense of their well-being in order to present a picture of children's lives. It found that the UK ranked in the bottom third of the country rankings for five of the six dimensions reviewed. While the UK ranked higher in the educational well-being dimension, it lagged behind in terms of relative poverty and deprivation, quality of children's relationships with their parents and peers, child health and safety, behaviour and risk-taking and subjective well-being. Shockingly, amongst the key findings, was the fact that the UK ranked amongst the worst in the developed world for children's well-being. A new report (UNICEF 2013) showed a slight improvement in the ranking with the UK placed at sixteenth overall out of the 29 countries surveyed, but this gives little reason for complacency.

The Children's Society's Good Childhood Inquiry which resulted in the report *A Good Childhood: Searching for Values in a Competitive Age* (Layard and Dunn 2009) showed that there is no strong or consistent relationship between per capita gross domestic product (GDP) and child well-being. The Czech Republic, for example, achieves a higher overall rank for child well-being than several much wealthier European countries. However, a relationship does exist between lower inequality and higher well-being. More equal societies, such as in Scandinavian countries, tend to do better on child well-being than less equal societies such as in eastern Europe or the UK.

Similarly, Wilkinson and Pickett (2010) describe possible links between economic deprivation and inequality with children's well-being. Their analysis of the evidence suggests that economic growth and increases in average income have ceased to contribute much to well-being in richer countries. They compare international data to emphasise that the prevalence of poor health and social problems in societies, which most people would agree is likely to undermine the well-being of the individual, is related to inequality rather than to average living standards. Wilkinson and Pickett (2010: 29) maintain that: 'Having come to the end of what higher material living standards can offer us, we are the first generation to have to find other ways of improving the real quality of life'.

We know that early childhood is a crucial time in the lives of young children and that there is much we can do to support and extend positive outcomes for all children and families. We also know that the contribution which early years provision can make to child well-being may be limited in terms of social and economic context. A setting in an economically deprived area, for example, can do nothing to meet the housing needs of families or contribute to family income. However, they can make a substantial contribution to the quality of life for individual children and families through anti-discriminatory practice and the fostering of self-esteem and positive dispositions to learning. Roberts (2010: 43) suggests 'We have seen an important expansion in the view of the curriculum itself [for early years], in which children's personal, social and emotional areas of development are all acknowledged'.

Waters (2009: 23) argues:

> Attending to children's learning dispositions and self-esteem in early years settings is a mechanism for supporting aspects of young children's well-being. Whether well-being is viewed as an intrapersonal trait or one that is socially mediated, supporting children's tendencies to respond positively to learning opportunities, their ability to respond with resilience to setbacks and their tendency to communicate effectively can be seen to be theoretically contributing to high levels of well-being.

Elfer and Dearnley (2007) argue that emotional well-being derives from feelings of security and being able to participate. In a recent (2010) seminar on well-being at London Metropolitan University, Peter Elfer identified three particular concerns or conclusions. The first is that it is a real challenge for nursery staff to be personally close enough to individual children in order to enable them to feel sufficiently thought about, whilst maintaining some professional distance. There is also the challenge of managing close emotional relationships with children whilst maintaining some professional distance, which although helped by emotional maturity is very difficult to manage systematically and over long periods, and perhaps unmanageable without organisational support. For Elfer, this third issue of organisational support means that the task of providing emotional closeness within a professionally accountable context should be made explicit and part of the setting ethos. In addition staff should be properly supported by trained managers and given time to engage in professional reflection both individually and in groups.

Practice example W1

At Stonebridge Children's Centre staff believe it is important to monitor the well-being of all children and to give them opportunities to talk about how they are feeling. At circle time children are encouraged to select a 'feelings' card and talk about why they are feeling a particular way that day. They also use the Leuven technique, developed by Ferre Laevers at University of Leuven (Belgium). He developed an Involvement Scale which aims to help adults see when children are deeply engaged with their learning.

Underpinning these conclusions is the idea that the well-being of children may be closely linked to the well-being of parents and other caregivers. Initial findings from the National Children's Bureau/London Metropolitan University Well-Being Project (Manning-Morton 2013), which consulted practitioners, students, academics, parents and children about their perceptions of well-being, highlight the same concern.

In summary a consideration of the well-being of young children brings into focus many important issues and considerations with regard to early years provision, policy, principles and practice. We know that early childhood is a crucial time in the lives of young children and that there is much we can do to support and extend positive outcomes for all children and families. Policy that reflects clarity of principles, purpose and a strong sense of direction will be needed, as well as a detailed analysis of the issues if we are to improve our child well-being record in the UK.

References

Anning, A. and Edwards, A. (2006), *Promoting Learning from Birth to Five: Developing Professional Practice in the Pre-school,* 2nd edn. Maidenhead: Open University Press.

Bronfenbrenner, U. (1979) *The Ecology of Human Development.* Harvard: Harvard University Press.

Elfer, P. and Dearnley, K. (2007) Nurseries and emotional well being: evaluating an emotionally containing model of continuing professional development, *Early Years* 27(3): 267–279.

Layard, R. and Dunn, J. (2009) *A Good Childhood: Searching for Values in a Competitive Age.* London: Sage.

Manning-Morton, J. (2013) *Exploring Well-being in the Early Years.* Maidenhead: Open University Press.

Pollard, E.L. and Lee, P.D. (2002) Child well-being: a systematic review of the literature, *Social Indicators Research*, 61: 59–78.

Roberts, R. (2010) *Well-Being from Birth.* London: Sage.

United Nations Children's Fund (UNICEF, 2007) *Child Well-being in Rich Countries: A Comparative Overview. Innocenti Report Card 7.* Florence: UNICEF Office of Research.

United Nations Children's Fund (UNICEF, 2013) *Child Well-being in Rich Countries: A comparative Overview. Innocenti Report Card 11.* Florence: UNICEF Office of Research.

Waters J. (2009) Well-being, in T. Waller (ed.) *An Introduction to Early Childhood*, 2nd edn. London: Sage.

Wilkinson, R. and Pickett, K. (2010) *The Spirit Level: Why More Equal Societies Almost Always Do Better.* London: Penguin.

World Health Organization (WHO, 1948) *Preamble to the Constitution of the World Health Organization as adopted by the International Health Conference.* New York, 19–22 June 1946; signed on 22 July 1946 by the representatives of 61 States (Official Records of the World Health Organization, no. 2, p. 100) and entered into force on 7 April 1948.

X

Xenophobia and xenoracism

The term xenoracism describes here negative and discriminatory attitudes towards people who are White. This might include Irish people, Jewish people, some refugees and asylum-seekers, and in recent years people who have migrated here from countries that have joined or will be joining the European Union.

Xenoracism often arises from xenophobia which is usually defined as a fear of strangers or 'foreigners'. In recent times, victims of xenoracism are often economic migrants who have come to the UK to make a better life for themselves, as with the recent influx of Polish workers. As with all forms of racism, xenoracism needs to be challenged as it generally arises from fear and ignorance and perceptions that jobs and housing are being threatened by an 'influx' of foreigners. The issues raised by xenoracism and the consequences for children are the same as for any form of racism and are explored earlier in this book.

Practice example X1

Bogdana is three and her family have just come from Romania to settle alongside other relatives in a small town in the UK. Nursery staff have noticed that Bogdana's mother seems isolated from the other parents and is reluctant to take part in the life of the setting. One day she arrives in tears and it emerges that she has been shouted at in the street and her family have been accused of taking jobs and accommodation away from other residents who are indigenous to the area. She explains that the family are staying with her husband's sister in overcrowded accommodation and that the casual farm work undertaken by her husband still has vacancies that have not been taken up.

The nursery staff do their best to support the family by celebrating Romanian culture and ensuring that measures to deal with any incidence of xenoracism in the setting are clearly set out in their policy and adhered to.

Y

Young children and identity

In many respects, identity formation is about deciding who we are in relation to other people, whether we are the same or different to them and how. This is a complex process because identities are usually constructed in relation to space and time. Individuals and groups have to negotiate the uncertainties of social change as well as the constraints that inequalities may place on them in order to develop a positive view of themselves, both as individuals and as part of the groups to which they feel they belong.

Young children themselves can be viewed as a subordinate group in society as they are subject to the limitations and restrictions of what adults think is desirable and appropriate. Moreover the dominant view of children and childhood derived from western psychology is that of the 'normal' child who lives in a world where they are economically and socially dependent on adults for everything. Arguably this ideal of the normal child, which has been created and sustained by experts in child development, is unhelpful when we consider that children must construct their identities in a fast-moving and fast-changing world where modern identities are often required to be complex and multifaceted.

Within a western developmental framework, issues of identity are static and unchanging. Children gradually acquire information about their true selves as they mature and grow into the roles that await them. But this idea of the normal child has been constructed from the values, beliefs and historical traditions of just this one group in society. Many believe that the consequences of this group's domination of the scientific, cultural, social and political worlds are that everything is judged from their norms.

What must be recognised, as Woodhead (1999) describes, is that all environments are culturally constructed, the product of generations of human activity and creativity, mediated by complex belief systems, including the 'proper' way for children to develop.

As Woodhead (1999: 38) observes: 'The most significant features of any child's environment are the humans with whom they establish close relationships'. After all, each one of us is a product 'of cultural history and circumstances' and this structures the kinds of care and education given to young children.

Researchers such as Woodhead have described the 'new childhood' in which the concept of the 'normal child' is seen as a construction rather than something that exists in reality. He suggests that there is not just one way of looking at childhood. Every society has expectations and norms about how children develop, how they learn and what their role is within their communities. In consequence, the western European and American (minority world) model of the child is only one way of describing and interpreting children's experiences. However, because of the dominance of the minority developed world view of the child – a view that is prevalent in the UK today – it is not surprising that this is thought to be the only way that children and childhood can be perceived.

This view of childhood as a social construction has led to an understanding that our ideas about what it is are always influenced by time, place, culture, class, gender, political and socio-economic conditions and agendas, and other complex interacting factors such as our own experiences of being a child.

Brooker and Woodhead (2008: 6) make the distinction between *personal identity* which refers to subjective feelings children may have about their own uniqueness and individuality, and *social identity* which is the need to belong and to be the same as others. For Brooker and Woodhead these represent 'two core human motives' whereby we need to feel we belong but also to feel that we are unique.

Identity is complex and fast changing in today's world. Consequently, as Dahlberg et al. (1999) argue, the role of the educator is not to enable a child to 'assume their true identity'; children are no longer predetermined to become farmers, housewives, soldiers or nurses. Instead, the educator has a role in supporting the child to explore all aspects of their identity:

> To live in a society that is characterised by postmodern conditions means that individual children have to adjust to a high degree of complexity and diversity, as well as continuous changes. In a more stable society the children's biography and knowledge were almost predetermined . . . much the same as their parents. In such conditions, the function of early childhood pedagogy can be understood as enabling children to assume their true identity, their essential identity, and the reproduction of knowledge and cultural values, predetermined earlier by religion and later by a supposedly value-free, objective science and reason.
>
> (Dahlberg et al. 1999: 54)

In today's complex world, therefore, the early years practitioner needs to recognise the skills required by children to negotiate the many roles and identities thrown at them. They can do this by building and reflecting on the cultural and social background of the child and family and seeing the early years setting as an extension of this. The key point is to make explicit how the expectations of others will influence how children choose to express themselves.

At the same time the practitioner must be alert to the barriers, either cultural or political, that may stop a child from adopting the identity they want. This may mean supporting the young boy who wishes to dress up in frilly and feminine clothes. Alternatively it may mean supporting a child of mixed parentage (with one Black and one White parent) to work out how they wish to be viewed by others and how they see themselves in a world where racial categorisation is seen as important.

Many children appear to be able to deal with various identities, each with its own value system and even its own language. They move comfortably between the worlds of home and family into the early years setting each with its own values and ascribed roles. Siraj-Blatchford and Clarke (2000: 3) rightly describe identity formation as 'a complex process that is never completed'.

For many of us the process of coming to know who we really are and what we are capable of is a lifelong process but the basis on which we come to understand and view ourselves is very likely to have been established when we were very young.

References

Brooker, L. and Woodhead, M. (2008) *Early Childhood in Focus 3. Diversity and Young Children: Developing Positive Identities*. Maidenhead: Open University.

Dahlberg, G., Moss, P. and Pence, A. (1999) *Beyond Quality in Early Childhood Education and Care: Postmodern Perspectives*. London: Falmer Press.

Siraj-Blatchford, I. and Clarke, P. (2000) *Supporting Identity, Diversity and Language in the Early Years*. Maidenhead: Open University Press.

Woodhead, M. (1999) Understanding child development in the context of children's rights, in C. Cunninghame (ed.) *Realising Children's Rights: Policy, Practice and Save the Children's Work in England*. London: Save the Children.

Z

Zenith
Zone of proximal development (ZPD)

Zenith

To be at the zenith is to be at the time when something is at its most powerful and successful. In recent years enormous strides have been made in the early years sector towards identifying and addressing barriers and achieving successful inclusive practice. These achievements have by and large been underpinned by policy, guidance and legislation. We have also witnessed the creation of an increasingly reflective, authoritative and professionalised workforce. Investment in people and infrastructure demonstrated that the importance and value of a robust and inclusive early years sector had begun to be recognised in real terms. This progress may be challenging to maintain in the present economic and political climate, as cuts to infrastructure, resources and policy changes all take their toll.

Research shows that we are living in an increasingly divided and unequal society. Direct links are being made between inequalities and later outcomes such as health, educational attainment and overall quality and length of life. Against this backdrop the early years sector still has the potential to be a pivotal and cost effective resource, as well as a powerful advocate for young children.

In the early years we recognise that it is the well-being of the children and families that we work with that is paramount. We know that there are many challenges ahead and that there is still an enormous amount of work to be done. Despite many positive and inspirational examples of practice we know that the early years sector is not yet at the zenith of inclusive practice. What is important here is that we continue to learn and grow in knowledge, skills and understanding about what it is possible for children to achieve and how we can best support them to have fulfilling lives.

Zone of proximal development (ZPD)

Vygotsky (1978) believed that the child is an active learner who develops various competencies without help. If helped by a 'more experienced other', however, children could 'perform' tasks at a higher level. He maintained that child development and learning do not occur in a vacuum, that is, other children and adults have a crucial role. For Vygotsky (1978) there are two developmental levels:

1. *The actual developmental level:* this is when the child can do something competently without help, e.g. build a tower.
2. *The zone of proximal development:* this is the gap between what a child can do without help and what they could do with help, e.g. the tower built unaided could become a castle with turrets.

In Vygotsky's own words (1978: 86):

> It is the distance between the actual developmental level as determined by independent problem solving and the level of potential development as determined through problem solving under adult guidance or in collaboration with more capable peers.

The concept of the zone of proximal development (ZPD) can be a useful and effective tool for those who teach and learn in a collaborative way and is sometimes described as the 'apprenticeship' approach. It has been a particularly useful concept in relation to children with learning disabilities who do not conform to prescribed ages and stages of development and ability.

In order to determine where a child is within the ZPD, practitioners must observe the child's unique learning style and acquire as much information as possible about them. From this information it should be possible to identify and track the child's current learning needs and the shifts in these needs as the child develops. As part of this process it is possible to determine and categorise what the child cannot yet do, what they can do with help, and what they can do alone.

There are four basic stages in the ZPD. In stage one, a child is aided by others such as practitioners, parents or peers on how to complete a task or understand a concept. In stage two, a child provides assistance to himself or herself. In stage three, a child internalises the method by which to complete a task or understand a concept. In stage four, a child goes back through the prior stages to learn a new task or concept.

An example would be reading a book with a child. Imagine they are reading the words of the book out loud to you as you follow along. They come across a word that is unfamiliar to them and ask you for help. Instead of directly telling them the word you show them pictures and ask questions about what they just read. They will eventually work out the word on their own and come to understand what it means. They will then learn to do it themselves first before asking for help.

The idea of matching tasks to children's current competencies to 'scaffold' their learning comes directly from Vygotsky's work which was later developed by Jerome Bruner. Bruner's theory of 'scaffolding' is similar to Vygotsky's concept of a 'zone of proximal development'.

Central to this theory is the idea that tasks that are set for the child need to be pitched at the right level. Tasks that are too difficult are outside the child's ZPD, and regardless of the amount of help in the form of scaffolding, the gap cannot be bridged. If the task is too easy the child will probably not be motivated. The ZPD approach is inclusive because not only does it require an individualised approach but it also encourages the use of collaborative learning strategies including that of peer to peer.

Photograph Z1 Tuning fine motor skills

Practice example Z1

Jacob, who is four, has been identified as having a 'global' delay' in his development which has resulted in a learning disability and difficulties with speech and communication. Staff have been using the Picture Exchange Communication System (PECS) in order to help develop his language and communication skills, but little progress has been made so far. There is a small tree in the nursery garden that children are sometimes allowed to climb, with adult support. Jacob indicates that he would like to do this too and he happily spends some time on a branch calling out to other staff and peers. When he comes down he rushes to the PECS cards and finds the symbol for 'tree'. Staff are able to use this breakthrough to encourage Jacob to identify the cards for 'drink' and 'puzzle', an activity which Jacob enjoys. Soon Jacob is using the PECS system effectively by himself to support his emergent speech and communication skills.

Reference

Vygotsky, L. (1978) Interaction between learning and development, *Mind in Society*, 9: 79–91.

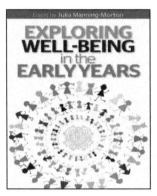

EXPLORING WELLBEING IN THE EARLY YEARS

Julia Manning-Morton

9780335246847 (Paperback)
October 2013

eBook also available

Children's experiences and well-being in their earliest years underpin and highly influence their future development and learning. Drawing on research with parents, children and a range of professionals in the early childhood field, this book considers how well-being is interpreted in the early childhood field. It includes snapshots of what our youngest children think about their well-being, and examines external environmental contexts that impact on well-being.

Key features:

- Focuses on appropriate pedagogical approaches and aspects of practice that support children's well-being
- Highlights the inseparability of adults' and children's well-being
- Prioritises children and families' socio-cultural contexts

www.openup.co.uk

A-Z OF PLAY IN EARLY CHILDHOOD

Janet Moyles

9780335246380 (Paperback)
2012

eBook also available

This indispensable guide uses a unique glossary format to explore some of the
key themes in play in early childhood, many of which regularly arise for students,
tutors, parents and practitioners. As well as covering key concepts, theories and
influential figures in the field, the book considers important aspects of each
construct and highlights the complexity of play in early childhood.

Key features:

- Split into a comprehensive glossary running through elements of play from
  A – Z, it is a useful, fun and unique companion to understanding children's
  play
- Original thoughts from well known early years people including Tricia
  David, Carol Aubrey, Angela Anning and Lilian Katz

www.openup.co.uk

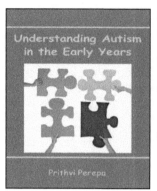

UNDERSTANDING AUTISM IN THE EARLY YEARS

Prithvi Perepa

9780335246649 (Paperback)
May 2013

eBook also available

This book provides an introduction to the autism spectrum and explores some of the theories and research which help in understanding the characteristics of young children who may be on the autism spectrum and the likely impact on their development and learning. It offers in-depth information on some of the key features which can lead to a child being diagnosed with autism and discusses the diversity of the spectrum, as well as presenting information on available screening tools.

Key features:

- Each chapter includes reflective activities which enable you to apply the information within your own context
- Key points and further sources of information are indicated at the end of each chapter
- Explores the role that early years practitioners have in supporting the child and helping them to develop appropriate communication and social skills

www.openup.co.uk

CONTEMPORARY ISSUES IN SPECIAL EDUCATIONAL NEEDS

Considering the Whole Child

David Armstrong and Garry Squires (Eds)

9780335243631 (Paperback)
2012

eBook also available

This thought- provoking and accessible book provides an overview of key issues in the education of children with Special Educational Needs and Disabilities. Written by highly experienced practitioners and educationalists, the book explores a range of approaches for working with this diverse group of learners and invites you to consider your possible responses.

Key features:

- Encourages the reader to make rich and useful connections between concepts and approaches 'out there' and their own experience and approaches in the classroom
- Explores some difficult and highly conceptual notions such as 'learner voice', 'diversity' or 'self-esteem' and what they actually mean in the context of complex and unique children with SEN
- Identifies the contributions psychology can make to developing and enriching educational practice

www.openup.co.uk

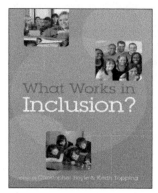

WHAT WORKS IN INCLUSION?

Christopher Boyle and Keith Topping

9780335244683 (Paperback)
2012

eBook also available

School inclusion is a perennially popular yet polemic topic in most countries.
This timely book explores what is known about inclusion, highlighting outstanding
examples of inclusion to provide a complete overview of successful inclusion.

The book concentrates on how to make inclusion work – from the view of
internationally established practitioners in the field of teacher education – with
a focus on what variables are likely to make a difference in practice.

Key features:

- Theories of inclusive education
- Examples of how inclusion can be encouraged and facilitated
- What prevents inclusion from being successful

www.openup.co.uk    OPEN UNIVERSITY PRESS
                          McGraw - Hill Education